RULES OF ENGAGEMENT

To our parents, Pat and Morys and Hilary and Michael,
who with over 90 years of marriage between them
have given us a role model and set the foundation
for us to build on.

KATHARINE AND RICHARD HILL

Rules OF *Engagement*

♥

HOW TO
PLAN A SUCCESSFUL WEDDING

♥

HOW TO
BUILD A MARRIAGE THAT LASTS

Text by Katharine and Richard Hill
Copyright © 2005 Care for the Family
Illustrations copyright © Kate Sheppard 2005

A Lion Book
an imprint of
Lion Hudson plc
Mayfield House, 256 Banbury Road,
Oxford OX2 7DH, England
www.lionhudson.com
ISBN 0 7459 4886 3

First edition 2005
10 9 8 7 6 5 4 3 2 1 0

Acknowledgments
pp. 17–21 Material provided by *Simple Extravagance Wedding Services*.
www.SimpleExtravagance.co.uk
pp. 53, 83–84, 108, 110 Extracts taken from *The Marriage Book* by
Nicky and Sila Lee published by Alpha International, 2002.
Used by kind permission of Alpha International.
pp. 107, 127 Extracts taken from *The Marriage Preparation Course
Manual* by Nicky and Sila Lee published by Alpha International, 2003.
Used by kind permission of Alpha International.

A catalogue record for this book is available
from the British Library

Typeset in 11.25/12 Lapidary 333
Printed and bound in Great Britain
by Cox & Wyman Ltd, Reading.

Contents

Acknowledgments

Writing this book together has been both a huge challenge and enormous fun.

We want to thank all at Care for the Family, especially Jonathan Booth and Dave Carlos, who believed in us enough to give us this project, and Rob Parsons for his wise advice, for writing the foreword and for giving us the title.

We also owe a huge debt of gratitude to Nicky and Sila Lee. We 'caught' our passion for marriage and family life from them and are grateful for their continued inspiration, support and encouragement.

We are very grateful to those couples who have allowed us to use their stories. We have changed their names to protect their privacy. The depth of experience that they and many others have shared with us over the years has given us a vast reservoir to draw from.

Thank you to Ross Cobb, Director of Music at Christ Church Clifton, Bristol, who helped us compile the suggested list of music for weddings. Many thanks also to Rachel McWalter from Simple Extravagance wedding planning service for sharing her expertise with us.

Thank you also to all those who have read through parts of the drafts, and given their comments and suggestions, and especially to Gail Ferguson and the team at Lion Hudson.

Finally thank you to our children, George, Charlotte, Edward and Henry, for giving up their time with us so we could write.

Foreword

Over the past twenty years or so, I have been privileged to speak to many thousands of people about marriage. Very often at the end of those seminars, queues of people wait to talk about their particular difficulties. I do my best, in the small amount of time available, to address their situation and point them in the direction of some longer-term help. They are sometimes in tears, but at the end of our conversation the couple take time to thank me for the marriage event they have just attended. And then every so often they pause and say, 'If only we'd heard some of this in the early years of our relationship.'

You are about to read this book because you are at the beginning of your relationship – a time for optimism, hope and the promise of good times ahead. But even if all your expectations are fulfilled, the truth is that you will go through some difficult times. In fact your love will never develop fully unless you face such times in your relationship and come through them together. When those times occur, it is important to realize that you are not alone: you are not the only couple in the world who are suddenly finding it hard to talk together, you are not the only ones in financial trouble and there are others who have found that a good sexual relationship sometimes take a little effort (someone once said, 'If a man wants a wild Friday night he had better begin working on it Monday morning!'). When we realize that it's not 'just us', it takes the pressure off and we can more easily find a way through. I love the way that *Rules of Engagement* enforces this truth; it's realistic, practical and not at all stuffy.

Foundations are important and this book will help you lay firm ones for your marriage. Starting with the myriad of things that have to be considered for the actual event – which, having just experienced my daughter's wedding, I believe to be on a par with running a small country – it considers the issues that you will face in the early years of your relationship. I urge you to work through the whole book. So many people spend years planning the wedding, but hardly a single day considering the issues they may have to face in the years of marriage that lie ahead. But you are not in that category, for you are taking time to make sure you never have to say, 'If only we'd heard that earlier.'

Let me take this opportunity to congratulate you not just on your marriage, but on your wisdom in taking a little time at the start of your lives together to strengthen the foundations on which you will build that marriage: in short, taking seriously the rules of engagement.

Rob Parsons,
Executive Director, Care for the Family

Introduction

If you have just got engaged, congratulations!

You are about to begin an exciting and wonderful adventure, but one which is not without its challenges. Our purpose in writing this book is to help you meet those challenges as they come along, beginning with the first challenge: planning your wedding. While planning a wedding is great fun, it will almost certainly be hard work. The same can be said of building a marriage.

We have been married for nearly twenty years. We love being married and count our marriage as one of our greatest achievements. However, looking back, we don't take one moment of it for granted. Like any worthwhile achievement, building a marriage can be costly. Nevertheless, we believe that there is no greater investment that we can make.

When you became engaged, it is likely that your decision was based on your love for each other and your desire to spend the rest of your lives together. You may be glad to know, however, that there are some other benefits to being married.

Research indicates that not only are married people happier but they are also healthier and have better prospects of employment. Marriage gives companionship; it forms the basis of family life and provides a safe, secure and stable environment within which to bring up children. As you begin to build your marriage together, not only will it benefit you, individually and as a couple, but also the communities in which you live and, therefore, society as a whole.

As you may have already discovered, organizing a wedding requires the strategic know-how and precision planning of the most complex military campaign! We hope therefore that the first section of *Rules of Engagement* will be of value as you organize your wedding day. It will help you to decide on your priorities, set a budget and plan the details accordingly. Most importantly, we hope it will help you keep your wedding day in perspective against the rest of your lives together.

The second part of the book contains ten 'rules of engagement', these being ten principles upon which to build your marriage. They are not intended as a restrictive set of regulations to tie you down but as tools to enable you to set each other free to fulfil your potential and to equip you for a marriage that will be significant and benefit generations to come.

The principal task of engagement is learning how to move from being single to being a couple, to thinking 'us' rather than 'I'. Building a strong marriage is not just about marrying the right person, however much we love them. It involves choice and commitment. It means acquiring skills and developing habits that will lay strong foundations for the future.

At the end of each section, you will find some exercises to enable you to discuss what you have read and to apply it to your relationship. We recommend that you work through these exercises with your fiancé(e), or together perhaps with another married couple who have some experience of the everyday ups and downs of married life.

Our hope is that, as you read this book together, you will develop a vision for your marriage. Perhaps you will discover new things about each other. Most importantly, we hope you have a lot of fun as you prepare to ride the roller coaster of married life. And that you will still be there for each other twenty, thirty, forty and even fifty years on.

PART 1

Planning the Wedding

THE ENGAGEMENT

George Bernard Shaw is quoted as saying, 'Like fingerprints all marriages are different.' Similarly, all proposals are different. Some are very simple, low key affairs, whereas others are much more flamboyant.

Jed proposed to Lucie by checking the tide times, getting up early in the morning and digging the words 'Will you marry me?' into the sand, to the delight and entertainment of others on the coastal path that morning. Andy proposed to Julie by giving her a large present which became a game of pass the parcel, each layer containing an object that symbolized an aspect of their love for each other.

However your proposal has taken place, it is unique to you and marks the beginning of planning your new life together.

The ring

The custom of giving and receiving rings traditionally symbolizes promises made and goods bestowed. We have friends who were on a very limited budget when they got engaged. The engagement ring was initially a curtain ring, replaced when they eventually saved some money. Personal preference as well as budget will dictate your choice but look around and consider all your options before buying. You may want a modern setting. Or you could consider buying an older ring from an antique market. The size and shape of your hands should also be taken into account. Those with long fingers can wear large rings; those with shorter fingers are generally better with something smaller and simpler. Unless you want to keep your engagement ring for special occasions, it is advisable to avoid a ring with a setting which looks as though it may catch on clothes or become scratched with wear.

Announcement

At one time it was customary for the bridegroom to ask his future father-in-law formally for permission to take his daughter's hand in marriage. Although this is no longer a formal requirement, many future grooms still do so out of courtesy. In any event, the first people to hear the good news should be both sets of parents. This might also be a suitable occasion to begin to discuss with them the timing and style of the wedding.

Some families still follow the tradition of placing a public announcement in the 'Forthcoming Marriages' column of a national or local newspaper. If you wish to do this, the announcement must be sent in writing and signed by one of the couple or a parent. Traditionally it is arranged and paid for by the bride's parents. (Suggested wording for the announcement can be found in Appendix 2.)

Engagement party

You might like to have a party to celebrate your engagement. This can be as formal or as informal as you wish. Some parents also like to host a party to celebrate. If they live some distance apart, they may even wish to organize separate celebrations.

Length of engagement

The length of an engagement is often dictated by practical considerations.

Luke and Ally were engaged for eighteen months to enable Ally to finish her course and complete her exams. Dave and Anna were married after an engagement of only four weeks because he was in the air force and given a posting abroad at short notice.

The availability of the church, register office or other approved venue, as well as the particular season of the year in which you want to marry, may also influence your choice. Having said that, as a general guide the average engagement is between five and twelve months. While you want to leave enough time to make the arrangements, too long an engagement can put a strain on your relationship.

WEDDING MYTHS

We hope what follows will help you navigate your way through the weeks ahead as you tackle the practicalities of your wedding. Many magazines and web sites will give you up-to-date information on what to buy and where to buy it, but we hope that the following pages will give you some general principles to bear in mind as you make plans together.

One of the delights of preparing couples for marriage is the number of weddings we are now invited to attend. Looking back, the most memorable weddings have been wonderful, not necessarily because of the great venue, grand reception or even the good food and drink. What has made them special has been the relaxed atmosphere and obvious love and enjoyment of the day by the bride and groom, encapsulated primarily in the way they say their vows to each other.

The following pages will help you to have a relaxed and memorable day and to keep the wedding arrangements in perspective against the backdrop of the rest of your lives together.

We want to begin by dispelling five myths that you may have been led to believe:

MYTH 1
You can have a perfect wedding
Settle for a wonderful wedding involving imperfect people.

MYTH 2
Your wedding day is for you and your fiancé(e)
Of course this is your special day but it is also an important day for at least two sets of parents and two or more families. If you can recognize this and learn to involve them in the arrangements, you will reap the benefits in the long term.

You are also hosting a celebration for your guests and it is a wonderful opportunity to show your appreciation for all they have done for you over the years. So when planning your day, give consideration to their needs as well as your own. (This is particularly important to bear in mind if your parents are contributing to the cost of the wedding.)

MYTH 3

The wedding industry has only your interests at heart

Visit any wedding fair and you will be inundated with the latest must-haves for the perfect wedding, many of which will involve you parting with a considerable amount of cash. There are of course many honest bridal businesses who sell beautiful things at a fair price. Just be aware that the wedding business is what it says – a business.

MYTH 4

Planning a wedding is glamorous and stress-free

If you plan carefully and stick to your budget, planning a wedding together can be fun. However, it is hard work and there will almost certainly be times when you have a difference of opinion either with each other or with your parents over the arrangements. Turn to *Rule 4, Find Joint Solutions* on page 73. Be realistic about what can be achieved within the time and budget available.

MYTH 5

You have to spend a fortune to have a fantastic wedding

It is quite possible to have a fantastic wedding on a limited budget. Be resourceful and use your common sense and initiative. Budget your time and money carefully and ask friends to help. (See page 48 for suggestions for cutting the cost.) Surf the web to find discount prices. Do your homework and be creative.

There is no doubt that planning a wedding can be a stressful business. Looking back, many couples have commented on how getting engaged seems to have catapulted them overnight into the exciting but all-consuming world of wedding planning. One couple said, 'The moment we got engaged, it felt like we had stepped onto a treadmill that was gaining speed and momentum and over which we had no control. We didn't know how to get off.'

Rachel McWalter, who runs the wedding planning service Simple Extravagance, advises couples to begin by pressing the 'pause' button. 'So many couples are pressurized into making expensive decisions without taking time to sit down and think through the type of wedding that they really want.'

So, before committing yourselves to any expenditure, set time aside to discuss and agree your priorities for the day. In particular, discuss whether you would like a church wedding or a civil ceremony. Then decide on the style of the reception and the number of guests. Try to be sensitive to the wishes of your respective families.

We suggest you use the following as a basis for discussion:

Agree values

Think about and discuss together:

1. Why do you want to get married?

2. Would you like a civil ceremony or a church wedding and why?

3. What part of the day do you think will be most special to you and why?

4. What do your parents expect from the day?

5. Why do you want others to share your day with you?

6. Who are you thinking of inviting?

On the basis of the above, complete the following:

Our values

The things that matter most to us about our wedding are:

1...

2...

3...

4...

5...

6...

If you can press the 'pause' button and agree your priorities for the wedding day, you will find your other decision making will fall into place within the framework you have set.

SETTING A BUDGET

Having discussed your values, the next task is to set an amount that is available for you to spend. If you are considering borrowing money, be realistic and only borrow what you can actually afford over a given period of time. Remember that your circumstances may well change and so will your needs. Of course you want your wedding day to be special but it might be wise to refrain from spending more money on that extra flower arrangement, chocolate fountain or stretch limousine if it means having insufficient money to buy a kitchen table or put a deposit on your first home.

Before committing yourselves to any expenditure, speak to family members about whether they would like to contribute to your wedding costs. If possible, determine when the money might be available. Then decide your overall budget for the wedding.

Having decided the amount that is available to spend, next consider setting a more detailed budget. As a rough guide, allocate:

50% to the reception	10% to photography
10% to attire	10% to stationery
10% to flowers	10% to extra items

Before you discuss actual figures, you may find it helpful first to establish what specific parts of your wedding to prioritize. This will provide you with guidelines for costing individual items of expenditure. In order to do this, turn to the Wedding Budget Planner (page 20) and in the first column assign a rating of between 1 and 3 to each item, according to its importance to you both where

1 = Very important

2 = Important

3 = Not important

For example, if you feel that wedding photographs are very important and would make all the difference to the wedding day and afterwards, you would rate wedding photographs 1. However, if you feel that a vintage wedding car would not be of importance to you, you would rate it 3.

In thinking through the importance of each item, you might discover that something you originally considered a priority is in fact not as important to you both as you had thought.

The next step is to complete the budget column by allocating the amount of money you anticipate spending. There will obviously be wide variations in the cost of each item but the amount you decide to spend in relation to your overall budget will directly relate to the level of importance that you have given it. To continue the example above, if you have rated the wedding photographs 1, this will mean spending a higher percentage of your budget on them, probably employing a professional photographer. However, if you had graded photographs as 3 in importance, you would direct that money to other priorities which might mean asking a friend to take photographs for you.

Some expenditure will be non-negotiable (for example, money already spent or fees for the ceremony). For most items, however, choices will need to be made and it may be necessary to bear in mind the Chinese proverb, 'If you do this, then you can't do that!'

While completing the Budget Planner, bear in mind your overall values for the day. For example, the amount of money allocated for the reception may allow you *either* an expensive sit-down meal for 50 *or* a finger buffet for 200. If one priority for the day is to share the occasion with as many friends as possible, that priority will dictate your choice. You may need to go back to your list and revise it as time goes on. Be warned. The issue is often not the individual item that is way outside your price bracket but the add-on effect of several items that are just beyond what you can afford.

If you are having difficulty in making a decision, you may find completing something like the following chart helpful in weighing up alternatives. The example given here is where to stay on the first night of the honeymoon.

	OPTION 1 Stay at reception venue	OPTION 2 Stay at a nearby B&B	OPTION 3 Stay at a good hotel nearby
For	No need to travel	Local Reasonably priced	Very special – would mark the occasion
Against	No formal 'going away' Other guests may be staying there	Not very special	Expensive
Cost	££	£	£££

Wedding Budget Planner

	Grade (1–3)	Budget	Cost
The engagement			
Ring(s)	....	....	....
Announcements/newspapers	....	....	....
Party	....	....	....
Photographs	....	....	....
Hen party	....	....	....
Stag party	....	....	....
Wedding preparation			
Invitations	....	....	....
Ring(s)	....	....	....
Attendants' presents	....	....	....
Best man's present	....	....	....
Ushers' presents	....	....	....
Parents' presents	....	....	....
Presents for each other	....	....	....
Wedding cake	....	....	....
Photographer	....	....	....
Video	....	....	....
Menus	....	....	....
Orders of service	....	....	....
Flowers for church	....	....	....
Flowers for reception	....	....	....
Bride's flowers	....	....	....
Bridesmaids' flowers	....	....	....

	Grade (1-3)	Budget	Cost

Outfits

Bride	....	....	....
Groom	....	....	....
Ushers	....	....	....
Attendants	....	....	....
Mother/mother-in-law	....	....	....
Father/father-in-law	....	....	....
Step-parents	....	....	....

The ceremony

Wedding venue hire	....	....	....
Fees for officiant	....	....	....
Music/organist	....	....	....
Heating	....	....	....
Guest book	....	....	....
Cars	....	....	....
Confetti	....	....	....

The main reception

Venue hire	....	....	....
Food	....	....	....
Drink	....	....	....
Entertainment	....	....	....

Party/evening reception

Venue hire	....	....	....
Food	....	....	....
Drink	....	....	....
Entertainment	....	....	....

Other

Honeymoon	....	....	....
Guest accommodation	....	....	....

TIPS FOR TAKING THE STRESS OUT OF PLANNING

1. Keep hitting the 'pause' button.

2. Don't feel pressurized into making decisions.

3. Remember your initial priorities – write them down and put them in a place where you will see them.

4. Keep the wedding in perspective.

5. Buy a wall planner and write down important dates.

6. Buy a folder with pockets to keep all the paperwork together.

7. Handle tasks in a sensible order. Focus on what needs doing, one step at a time.

8. Plan the ceremony. Then make the difficult and expensive decisions, e.g.

Reception + number of guests

Colour scheme/Tone for the day

Bridal outfit

Bridesmaids' dresses

Groom's outfit

Photography

Cars

Stationery

Flowers

9. Try to be sensitive to your families' wishes.

10. Build some planning-free zones into your diary, such as going

out for a meal with your fiancé(e) and agreeing not to mention the wedding.

11. Buy some fizz or party poppers to remind you that this is a celebration. Crack open the fizz and pull the party poppers if you're feeling stressed!

THE WEDDING PLANNER CALENDAR

Each November we buy a magazine which, as well as giving very impractical advice on how to make your own evergreen swags or individual Christmas puddings for twenty, also provides an easy-to-follow Christmas planner. As an aide-memoire it is invaluable and prevents us from forgetting to ice the Christmas cake before 11.00 p.m. on Christmas Eve.

We hope that the following planner will be of similar use as a general guide. Please ignore the suggestions that are not relevant to you. Add your own ideas as well. Some individual subjects are dealt with in slightly more detail in the next section, 'The A–Z of Planning a Wedding'.

It is quite possible to arrange a wedding in a few weeks. We have used six months as the average starting point but you can adapt the timings to suit your individual circumstances.

At any stage remember to hit the 'pause' button.

Six to three months before

1. Plan the type of wedding and number of guests.

2. Choose the date, time and place for the ceremony.

3. Arrange to see the minister or registrar.

4. Find out about and attend a marriage preparation course (contact NCSN@cff.org.uk for details of a course near you).

5. Set a budget.

6. Choose and book the venue for the reception.

7. Organize the catering: either book professional caterers or arrange for friends to help.

8. Order your wedding cake, arrange for a friend to make it or plan to make your own.

9. If you want live music, book or arrange it now.

10. Order the wedding cars or arrange to borrow them from friends.

11. Choose and book a photographer.

12. Choose and book a florist or arrange for friends to help provide flowers.

13. Choose and invite attendants – bridesmaids, pageboys, best man and ushers. Invite anyone else you would like to take part in the service.

14. Bride: begin thinking about your wedding dress. Consider whether you want to buy, hire, borrow or have one made.

15. Groom: consider what you will wear and order it if necessary.

16. Choose and order or arrange the making of dresses, outfits and accessories for the attendants.

17. Decide where to go for your honeymoon and make reservations. (Arrange somewhere nearby for the first night at least.)

18. Order or design and make your wedding invitations (see Appendix 3).

Three to two months before

1. Discuss and plan your wedding music (see Appendix 10).

2. Discuss and plan the wedding service or ceremony, including appropriate readings (see Appendices 8 and 9).

3. Discuss the order of service with the minister or the ceremony with the registrar. Place an order for or make the orders of service (see Appendix 6).

4. Agree a date for the wedding rehearsal and notify all the people involved.

5. Order any additional stationery, e.g. place cards, cake boxes.

6. Discuss and agree menu with caterers if appropriate.

7. Discuss and arrange for the provision of any necessary road signs or extra parking facilities.

8. Choose and buy your wedding ring(s).

9. Plan and organize a list of wedding presents. (Most large department stores operate a wedding gift register.)

10. Make an appointment to see your doctor or family planning clinic if necessary.

11. If you are planning to go abroad for your honeymoon, arrange any necessary inoculations. Obtain any necessary visas.

12. Check your existing passports are in order. Organize a passport in the bride's new married name if you wish.

13. Buy any necessary clothes for going away and for your honeymoon. Buy or decide upon the shoes you will be wearing on the day.

14. Research accommodation options for those travelling to the wedding from a distance.

Eight to six weeks before

1. Finalize your guest list and send out invitations. Keep a record of replies.

2. Meet with the florist and select flowers.

3. Buy presents for the bridesmaids, best man and any other attendants.

4. Make arrangements for where any bridesmaids or pageboys will dress on the day of the wedding.

5. Check that all licences, banns and certificates are in order for the ceremony.

6. If you are marrying in church, go to hear your banns read.

Four weeks before

1. Bride: have a final fitting for your wedding dress, wearing the shoes you will wear for the ceremony. It is also a good idea to wear the shoes around the house so they are comfortable on the day.

2. Make a provisional seating plan for the reception if appropriate.

3. Check that there will be a room at the reception available for you to change.

4. Bride: discuss ideas for your hair with a hairdresser or find a friend who will help you. Try the style out beforehand. Try out your make-up.

5. Organize the stag night and the hen party.

6. Groom: begin to think about and write speech.

7. Arrange separate gatherings for bride's and groom's families, if appropriate, for the night before the wedding.

Two weeks before

1. Confirm arrangements for photographs, flowers, cars and catering.

2. Assemble clothes and other items for honeymoon.

3. Check that any table decorations, linen and place cards are in order.

One week before

1. Give final numbers to caterer.

2. If required, send wedding announcement to newspaper.

3. Wrap gifts for attendants.

4. Bride: arrange a facial, manicure, pedicure or any other relaxing treatment if you wish.

5. Pack honeymoon luggage. Check tickets. Give tickets and spare car keys to best man.

6. Attend the wedding rehearsal if appropriate.

7. Make arrangements for your clothes to be taken home from the reception after the wedding.

The day before

1. Fill car with petrol. Check oil, water and tyres.

2. Pack going-away clothes and have suitcase(s) delivered to reception.

3. If there will not be time on the day, give presents to attendants.

4. Hold a family party the night before.

5. Get a reasonably early night.

The day

Relax and enjoy!

Tips for enjoying the day

1. Allow yourselves plenty of time to get ready.

2. Don't 'sweat the small stuff' (i.e. don't let small issues spoil the day).

3. Be your own internal camera – make yourselves pause every so often to take in and remember each stage of the day.

THE A–Z OF
PLANNING A WEDDING

While you may want to read this section through, it is designed as a reference section for you to dip into and return to as necessary.

🌿 Accessories

The right accessories can beautifully enhance your wedding dress. Even if you are not wearing a veil, most brides choose to have flowers in their hair, either attached to a headdress or woven in singly. You may prefer to wear a hat to complete your outfit, especially if you are not wearing a traditional wedding dress. Shoes need to be comfortable and non-slip with a heel to suit your dress and height. The groom, best man and ushers may choose to wear coordinating ties or waistcoats.

🌿 Accommodation

It is helpful to research local hotels or bed and breakfasts for guests travelling any distance. You might include a list of options at varying prices with the invitations, giving web sites or contact numbers.

🌿 Approved premises

It is possible to have the wedding ceremony and reception in approved premises such as a castle, mill, tithe barn or stately home. Your local register office will be able to give you a brochure listing the options available in your area. Select the venue where you wish to marry, check the availability of the registrar and book them together.

A proposed change in the law means that it is likely that in the near future you will be able to marry at any venue, provided an 'approved person' (legal or religious celebrant) conducts the ceremony.

🌿 Attendants

The custom of having attendants at a wedding is a practical one. Traditionally, older bridesmaids were there to help prepare and dress the bride for her wedding day. Many bridal parties are now made up of one or two older bridesmaids, together with younger bridesmaids or pageboys. A bride will often ask a sister, friend, nephew, niece or godchild to take part in this way. If you plan to involve very young children as attendants you may need to be flexible as to what they are able (or prepared) to do on the day itself.

🦋 Banns

If you decide to marry in the Church of England, you will need to have your banns read. Banns are the public announcement of your intention to marry. They are read out in the churches of the parish where each of you live for three consecutive weeks before the wedding and are valid for three months. There will be a small fee. Once they have been read out, the vicar will give you a banns certificate.

If you want to marry in a church other than your local parish church, you will need to obtain a common licence or, in exceptional circumstances, a special licence. Your minister will tell you how to apply if necessary.

🦋 Best man

The best man carries considerable responsibility for assisting the groom on the wedding day. Grooms generally choose a brother or a close friend. The best man helps the groom arrange the stag night. He looks after the ring(s) during the service and may also have custody of the honeymoon tickets and passports. He sits with the groom during the service and sees that everyone has transport to the reception. At the reception, it is the best man's role to make a speech and to reply on behalf of the bridesmaids.

🦋 Bridesmaids

Traditionally, bridesmaids are unmarried (a married bridesmaid is called a matron of honour). The bridesmaids follow the bride and, if appropriate, help with her train. We have been at weddings where the bride has (once in error and once planned) followed the bridesmaids into the church. The chief bridesmaid may look after any younger bridesmaids or pageboys and holds the bride's flowers during the ceremony, returning them to her usually during the signing of the register. Either she or the bride's mother may help the bride to change and may also look after the wedding dress if the reception is being held away from home. It is usual for the bride to choose the bridesmaids' dresses. The style will depend on that of the wedding and of the bride's dress in particular. If bridesmaids are of different ages, one option is to choose a particular fabric and have all the bridesmaids' dresses made in it to styles that suit the individuals. Although traditionally bridesmaids' dresses are paid for by the bridesmaids themselves, today the cost is often shared.

🎬 Cake

The wedding cake forms the centrepiece at the reception. Traditionally it is a rich fruit cake, iced and decorated, which may have two, three or four tiers. Some couples keep the top tier and use it as the christening cake for their first child. Although fruit cake is traditional, many couples choose a chocolate or plain sponge cake instead or as well. The bride and groom generally cut the first slice of cake before the toast and speeches. The rest of the cake is then sliced and served after the speeches. Many people like to send a slice of cake to anyone who has been unable to come to the wedding and cake boxes can be ordered for this purpose. You can order a cake from a professional baker or arrange for a friend to make one for you. The possibilities for decorating the cake to suit the style of the wedding are many and varied. Specialist magazines will give you ideas. If your budget is limited, a cake can be purchased from a large department store or supermarket and decorated appropriately.

🎬 Catering

The size, type and time of your reception (and of course your personal preference) will all influence your choice of food. If you are using professional caterers for your reception, go through the menu carefully with them and let them know of any special dietary requirements for your guests. If you are not using professional caterers and are holding a small reception, you might consider asking a friend to help or inviting guests to contribute dishes. It is advisable to choose simple dishes that you think most people will enjoy.

🎬 Ceremony

Take as much care over planning the wedding ceremony itself as you do in planning the rest of the day's activities, whether you are marrying in a church, register office or other approved venue. You might want to consider involving others in the service by asking them to take specific roles in the readings, prayers or music (see Appendices 8, 9 and 10 for suggested readings and music).

If you are marrying in a church where you are already part of the church family, the wedding service can be a great celebration of your individual lives being joined together in God.

If you choose to marry in a licensed venue, regulations stipulate that nothing with religious connotations can be incorporated into the ceremony.

✵ Children

When compiling a guest list, many brides and grooms agonize over whether to include children in the invitation. You may want to include all close family members but most parents will understand if children are not invited. If you do decide to invite a number of young children, it is a good idea to provide some specific entertainment for them, such as a bouncy castle or video room which will ensure both they and their parents enjoy the day to the full.

✵ Church weddings

If you decide to marry in church, the first thing you need to do is to arrange to see the vicar or parish priest and ask if they will conduct your wedding.

Marriage in the Church of England or Church in Wales: you will be able to marry in a church where you are on the electoral roll or where either or both of you live in the parish. The vicar will arrange either for your banns to be called on three consecutive Sundays before the day of your wedding or for a common licence to be issued (see Banns). The marriage will also be registered by the vicar so there is no need to involve the superintendent registrar. A fee will need to be paid.

Marriage in any other church or religious building: A registrar's certificate or licence to marry needs to be obtained for every marriage according to any other denomination or faith other than the Church of England (see Civil Ceremony). The church or religious building must normally be in the registration district where either or both of you live. If the church does not have its own registrar, you will need to arrange for the registrar to attend the service. There will be a prescribed fee for this.

✵ Civil ceremony

You may decide on a civil ceremony, either in a register office or in another building approved for civil marriage. The ceremony in the register office will be much shorter and simpler than a church service and the number of guests you can invite will be limited by the space available. Ceremonies in approved premises can be personalized to suit you; again, the number of guests will be determined by the size of the premises. All marriages must be witnessed by at least two adults.

If you choose a civil ceremony, you may marry at any register office or approved premises that you choose. You need to:

i) contact the superintendent registrar of the district where you intend to marry;

ii) make arrangements at the venue in question (if not a register office);

iii) also give formal notice of marriage to the superintendent registrar of the district *where you live*.

Both of you must have lived in a registration district for at least seven days immediately before giving notice at the register office. If you both live in the same district, you should attend your local register office together to give your notices of marriage. There will be a fee for this, details of which can be obtained from the superintendent registrar. If you live in different registration districts, each of you will need to give notice in your own areas. After giving notice, there must be an interval of a further fifteen clear days before the registrar issues the certificate and the marriage can take place. (For example, if notice is given on 1 April, the marriage may take place on or after 17 April.)

The notice of marriage is valid for one year. If you have a long engagement, many register offices run a provisional booking system which means that you can book more than a year in advance if you wish. You can then go ahead and book the reception and simply give your legal notice of marriage at the appropriate time to confirm the booking.

Because the notice is a legal statement, you must give notice in person. A relative or friend may not give notice on your behalf, nor may it be done by telephone. Most register offices have an appointment system. When giving notice of marriage, you will need to produce proof of your identity and nationality (for example, birth certificate and passport). If you are divorced, you will need to show a decree absolute bearing the court's official stamp. If you have been widowed, you will need to bring a certified copy of your spouse's death certificate. Also, if you have changed your name, the relevant documentation will need to be shown. Additionally, if either of you is under eighteen, the registrar will need proof that a parent or guardian consents to the marriage.

If either of you is divorced, you may choose to have a civil ceremony followed by a church service of blessing (see Invitations, Appendix 4). Whether you can marry in church in these circumstances depends on the policy of the church in question. Most ministers like to talk to you about the past to help you make a new start (see *Rule* 6 for those undertaking a second or subsequent marriage).

❋ Confetti

Many churches or register offices will have guidelines about where it is possible to throw confetti. They may make an announcement about this before the arrival of the bride. Flower petals or crushed lavender make an attractive alternative.

❋ Dress

Bride: choosing a dress can be very easy or very difficult, depending on how precise an idea you have of the style you want. The traditional wedding dress is white and floor-length but you can choose whatever style you like. Remember that during the service it is the back of the dress that will be seen. It is a good idea to have a detachable train, designed so it can be hooked up for the reception. If you are being married in a register office, you may prefer to wear a shorter dress or suit. You can buy your dress ready-made or have it made for you, either professionally or by a friend. Alternatively, if you are gifted in this area, you may be able to make your own dress. If you are on a limited budget, consider buying an end-of-line sample, hiring or buying a second-hand dress off the internet. Arrange a fitting wearing the shoes that you plan to wear on the day.

Groom: for a formal wedding, a groom will often wear traditional morning dress or, for a late afternoon wedding, a dinner jacket, both of which may be hired. Alternatively, an ordinary suit is fine. The important thing with dress is to check the expectations of each family.

The best man and other close family members usually take their lead from the groom. If you are in the armed services, you may wear your uniform. Plain black, lace-up shoes look good with most suits. If you buy new shoes, remember to wear them in so that they are comfortable on the day.

Drink

Champagne and sparkling wine are the traditional drinks to serve at a wedding. For receptions with a sit-down meal, consider serving red or white wine with the food and a non-alcoholic alternative. A glass of champagne or sparkling wine may be given to guests on arrival and also before the toasts. If you are doing your own catering, many retailers provide free glass hire if you buy the wine from them. If the venue allows you to provide your own drink, consider a sale-or-return arrangement and take into account any corkage charges.

Where professional caterers are supplying the wine, make sure that you agree a price and taste it beforehand. Alternatively, you can just serve soft drinks, in which case a fruit punch, such as elderflower cordial with mint and slices of lemon, can make a good alternative. If you have a limited budget, you might consider a paying bar in the evening.

Entertainment

If your reception is in the evening, you may want to organize music and dancing. This can be live or recorded music. A barn dance or ceilidh is also great fun and ensures that most guests can participate.

Evening reception

If you have friends that you have been unable to include in the main reception, consider inviting them to the service and then to a later evening reception after the main reception has finished. Another way of including more friends is to invite everyone to the speeches and cake cutting immediately after the ceremony. A selection of guests then moves on to a smaller reception. In this case, separate invitations need to be issued (see Appendix 5).

Flowers

When choosing flowers, think carefully about where they will be most noticed and appreciated by your guests. It is surprisingly easy to overrun your budget in this area. If you are using a florist, ask to see photographs of their work or find one who comes with a personal recommendation. When you meet the florist, take along swatches and a sketch of your dress plus a small piece of material or ribbon from the bridesmaids' dresses. If a friend is arranging your flowers for you, discuss with them in detail what you would like. The style and shape of the bride's bouquet will be partly dependent on the design and style of her dress. Similarly, consider size – a petite bride would be dwarfed by an enormous bouquet while a tall bride may look odd with a very small posy. Small posies of fresh flowers are also suitable for young children to carry.

As well as the bride's bouquet and headdress, you will need to consider flowers for the bridesmaids, buttonholes for the groom, father of the bride, best man and ushers, flowers for the church and flowers for the reception. Potted plants can sometimes be hired for the day from local nurseries and marquees can be decorated with hanging baskets. If you are getting married in a season when flowers are more expensive, consider using artificial flowers mixed with real foliage and the occasional spray of fresh flowers. If you use real flowers, consult the table in Appendix 7 and try to obtain flowers that are in season. Whatever flowers you decide on, ensure your arrangements are in keeping with the venue and style of the day.

🌿 Gift list

Wedding guests very much appreciate having a wedding list from which to choose a gift. Most department stores operate a wedding register where gifts can be bought in person, on the telephone or on line. There are also dedicated wedding-list companies. Alternatively, it is possible to produce your own list. Compiling a list is quite time-consuming but it ensures that people give you what you really need and avoids duplication. If possible, choose gifts in the widest possible price range and keep a note of all you receive so you can write thank-you letters. If gifts are brought to the reception, arrange for the best man or bride's mother to be responsible for them.

🌿 Hen party

A hen party is generally organized by close friends of the bride. It should take place at least two weeks before the wedding and can take any form from a day at a spa or health farm to an afternoon shopping followed by a pizza and video. It is often arranged to take place at the same time as the groom's stag party. The costs are generally divided between the group.

🌿 Homecoming

It is worth some planning and some help from friends to ensure that when you arrive back from your honeymoon not only is the electricity and water connected but there is some food in the fridge and sheets on the bed. When you are tired from travelling, this can make all the difference.

🌿 Honeymoon

Remember that you will be tired after the wedding so it is sensible to stay somewhere locally for the first couple of nights in order to recover and then travel further afield if you plan to do so. An energetic water sports holiday or a trek across the foothills of the Himalayas may not be the best honeymoon choice. If you want to have the trip of a lifetime, plan it a year or so into marriage. Decide whether to honeymoon in this country or abroad and whether you want a hotel or self-catering accommodation. The more you find out about your destination, the less chance of your being disappointed. Book ahead where possible, as leaving too much to chance can be stressful. Where possible, a personal recommendation is invaluable.

Remember to specify that you want a double bed; it is worth saying when you book that it is for your honeymoon. Most hotels will try to give you a good room and some will even offer flowers or sparkling wine. Remember also to allow some spending money in your budget. If travelling abroad, you may need to order currency. Take out insurance and check that your passports and any visas are in order. If the bride would like to change her name on her passport, a form can be obtained in advance from the post office for this purpose. Of course you want your honeymoon to be wonderful but do be realistic and don't let small imperfections spoil your time together.

✵ Insurance

As with most areas of life, it is possible to insure a wedding. This will cover eventualities such as theft, cancellation of the reception due to illness or double-booking of the venue. Consider also taking out travel insurance for the honeymoon.

✵ Invitations

The invitations should be sent from the home of the bride's parents six to eight weeks before the wedding. Formal invitations are usually printed. Printers, department stores and large stationers hold sample books of designs to suit all tastes and budgets. It is also possible to buy packs of preprinted invitations to be completed as appropriate after purchase.

It is increasingly common for a couple to design their own invitations on computer. An informal invitation needs to contain the same information as a formal invitation but there is more choice, both in what may be said and how to say it, as well as in the appearance of the invitation in terms of colour and illustration. (For appropriate wording, see Appendices 3, 4 and 5.)

Along with the invitations, you may wish to enclose a response card, a map and directions to the ceremony, details of accommodation and the gift list.

🦋 Jewellery

It is worth considering in advance what jewellery the bride and bridesmaids will wear that will complement their dresses.

🦋 Legal matters

The definition of a legal marriage is the union of one man with one woman, voluntarily entered into for life to the exclusion of all others. You must be over 18, or over 16 with your parents' written consent, and legally free to marry. A marriage may take place on any day at any time between 8 a.m. and 6 p.m. in a registered place of worship, a register office or other approved premises. Civil or ecclesiastical preliminaries (banns, licence or superintendent registrar's certificate) must precede every marriage.

🦋 Make-up

It is a good idea for brides to practise applying their make-up before the day itself. It might be wise to put make-up on after putting on the dress, perhaps protecting the dress with a scarf.

🦋 Marriage preparation

By attending a marriage preparation course during the months leading up to your wedding, you will be ensuring that you are preparing not just for the wedding day but for your future together. If the registrar or minister does not offer you marriage preparation, contact The National Couple Support Network at Care for the Family, PO Box 488, Cardiff, CF15 7YY, tel: (029) 2081 1733. Alternatively, email NCSN@cff.org.uk who will try to put you in touch with a course in your area.

🦋 Music

Church wedding: if you are getting married in church, it is worth spending time and care choosing the music for the service. You should discuss your choice with the minister. Depending on the church's tradition, there are usually a number of options, such as a formal choir, organ music or a band. It is worth choosing hymns and songs that most people know. You will also need to choose music for the entrance of the bride and for when you both leave the church, as well as music to play during the signing of the register. (Some suggestions are contained in Appendix 10.)

Civil ceremony: music for a civil ceremony must not contain any religious reference. Either modern or classical music may be played (live or recorded) when entering and leaving the marriage room. Both the selection of music and where it is to be played should be agreed in advance with the superintendent registrar. It would also be wise to check that suitable equipment to play music is available.

New name

At the end of the ceremony, the bride signs her maiden name in the register. Taking a new name is optional and some women choose to retain their maiden name for a number of purposes. The acquisition of a new name is one of the most visible signs of a new marital status. If you are changing your name, the following checklist will remind you to inform the right people:

1. Driving licence
2. Bank accounts – you may also wish to open a joint account
3. Building society
4. Credit card companies
5. Your employer/benefit office
6. Life insurance and pension scheme
7. Tax office
8. Passport

Order of service

This can be printed professionally or produced on a home computer. The style of the wedding invitation may be replicated in the order of service. It is customary to include the names of everyone taking part in the service, not only the minister but also those of friends or family who are giving readings or leading prayers. If you would like to invite another minister to take part, you should ask the resident minister's consent.

Hymns can be printed in full but you need to check whether you need permission for the copyright. Ask the minister if there is a specific music copyright licence number: if so, include the completed phrase 'All music is covered by CCL no. …' at the bottom of the page.

Otherwise the appropriate address to write to for this information generally appears in the acknowledgments in the front of the hymn book. In many cases no fee is required, provided you print an acknowledgment in the order of service.

Remember to order one order of service per person plus some spare copies as you might like to send a copy to anyone unable to be there on the day.

🎀 Photography

The cost of the photography at your wedding can constitute a large part of the wedding budget and it is worth taking time and care considering your options as the pictures will be the tangible memory of the day. Ideally, get a personal recommendation, ask to meet the photographer and look at their work. In the absence of a personal recommendation, you can check whether they are a qualified member of the MPA (Master Photographers Association), BIPP (British Institute of Professional Photographers) or Guild of Wedding Photographers. Discuss beforehand in detail what you want from the photography. You may wish to have a reportage style documentary of your day or more formal photographs. Either way, ensure that all key family members are included.

Check exactly what the photographer is offering in the way of prints, albums or on-line ordering. Find out the cost of extra prints and reprints. Remember that whatever price you agree with the photographer, you will almost certainly want to order more prints than you anticipated. Check that the photographer you meet will be the one who turns up on the day and that they have insurance and back-up equipment. Also check with the minister or registrar whether any pictures may be taken during the ceremony. The majority of photographs will almost certainly be taken after the ceremony and at the reception. Consider also whether you would like the photographer to come to the house to photograph the bride getting ready.

If the majority of photographs are taken on arrival at the reception, do consider the needs of your guests and offer them a drink while other photographs are being taken. Similarly, remember to offer the photographer refreshment if they are there all day. If your budget does not run to an official photographer, consider choosing a friend or friends with some experience and make sure they know what is expected of them. Do bear in mind, however, that it is quite a responsibility to be asked to take photographs at a friend's wedding. Another idea is to put disposable cameras on each table for guests to use during the reception and leave behind for you to develop.

Pictures taken on your honeymoon are also an important part of the record of your wedding, so remember to pack a camera and plenty of film.

✳ Post-wedding blues

After all the excitement and build up to the wedding, it is not uncommon to feel let down on return from honeymoon and to struggle to readjust to normal life. 'I got married last October and I'm confronting wedding withdrawal. It's been hard to kick the high of the

bridal habit and to put away my wedding dress and veil for ever. But what goes up must come down. It's the law of fiancé(e) physics.' (*Wedding Day Magazine*, February/March 2004)

Adjusting to married life and building foundations for the future is fun but can be hard work. Work through the Rules in the second half of this book and understand how to build a relationship that will last a lifetime. Try to understand and meet each other's needs, make special time together and seek help if you need it. Use the memories of your wedding day as a springboard to the future (and brides don't have to put their wedding dress and veil away immediately).

🎥 Quantities

The type of reception you are having will influence both your choice of food and drink and the quantity you will require.

For an informal buffet, allow between 10 and 15 finger food items per head. There should be a variety of food. If the guest list numbers between 50 and 100, allow a choice of eight to ten different dishes. If the guests number 250 or more, provide about 20 different sorts of food.

As a general rule, you should allow half to three-quarters of a bottle per head of wine, sparkling wine or champagne for an afternoon reception. Remember that guests will drink more on a hot day.

As a rough guide:

Coffee – 450g ground coffee or 125g instant coffee makes 60 cups

Tea – 125g makes 60 cups

Soft drinks – 6 drinks to a litre

Beer – 4 drinks to a litre

Champagne or wine – 6 glasses per bottle

🎥 Receiving line

Where there is a formal receiving line, the bride and groom line up with both sets of parents to greet the guests individually as they arrive at the reception. Alternatively, you may decide that only the bride and groom receive the guests or you may opt for no receiving line at all.

🎥 Reception

The choice of location for your reception will depend on the number of guests, the atmosphere you wish to create and whether it is to be a formal or informal occasion. You may wish to hold the reception in your own home or, if you have the space, in a marquee in your garden. A rough estimate of space required is one square metre per person. A church or village hall is often a good choice and lends a community feel to the celebration. Most large hotels are available for wedding receptions or you may wish to consider somewhere more unusual, perhaps a canal boat or a castle or other historic building. Visit the places you are considering and obtain written estimates to enable you to compare costs and make up your mind.

✖ Rehearsal

The minister, or whoever is conducting your service, may suggest a date for a wedding rehearsal in the week prior to the wedding. This is a good opportunity to go through the ceremony and clarify any queries you may have. You need only wear casual clothes for this. Practise walking up the aisle *slowly*: many people walk too fast because they are nervous.

✖ Rings

The exchange of engagement and wedding rings continues a tradition that began thousands of years ago. Engraved betrothal rings existed in medieval times. Gold is the traditional metal for engagement and wedding rings. It is mixed with other metals to give it strength and is classified according to the quantity of pure gold in the ring. The purest is 22 carat; 18 carat is less expensive and more hardwearing; and 9 carat contains the least gold. Platinum is another hardwearing metal that is suitable for a wedding ring.

Have your ring size measured properly at any jewellers. Remember that brides will wear their engagement and wedding rings together so choose rings of the same metal and try them on together to make sure that they fit well and do not rub. The groom often chooses a wedding ring to match the bride's or occasionally a signet ring instead. It is a good idea to order your rings eight to ten weeks before the wedding in case they need alteration. You may also wish to have them engraved on the inside with the wedding date, your initials or a personal message.

✖ Seating

The seating arrangements again reflect the formality of the occasion. If you are serving cake or canapés, guests may stand throughout. At an informal buffet, guests may wish to choose where they sit in groups at small tables. A sit-down reception requires a seating plan and place names. This will involve a considerable amount of work and probably cannot be finalized until the day before the wedding. Take care to put guests at a table with at least some people that they know, as it will add to their enjoyment of the day. Nowadays many brides and grooms choose to sit among their guests. However, if you have a top table, the conventional arrangement is to sit the wedding party facing the guests and next to each other as follows:

Bridesmaid

Groom's father

Bride's mother

Groom

Bride

Bride's father

Groom's mother

Best man

Depending on your family circumstances, the order may need to be adapted. It may be more appropriate to arrange for each parent to host a table of their own.

🎋 Speeches

There is a traditional order to speeches at the reception. These are normally given at the end of the meal, although it is quite feasible to have them before the meal begins. The bride's father or a family friend makes the first speech and proposes a toast to the bride and groom. The groom then replies and thanks the bride's parents for the wedding and for their daughter. He can also thank his own parents and all others who have contributed to the special day. He then proposes a toast to the bridesmaids. The best man then replies on behalf of the bridesmaids. There are many books on the market giving advice on speech-making. A golden rule is to remember the range of guests and to be careful to avoid giving offence when using humour.

🎋 Stag night

The stag night is generally organized by the best man and groom and is a chance for the groom's bachelor friends to give him a good send-off. The stag night should take place at least two weeks before the wedding and might in fact be simply a night out or an entire weekend of sport and entertainment. As with the hen night, the cost is generally shared among the group.

✳ Table decorations

Depending on the style of the reception, tables can be decorated to follow a theme. Where the budget is limited, a single flower or a candle looks attractive. If you plan to have something more elaborate, keep any decorative arrangement on the table either low or very high so your guests can speak to each other without having to peer through hedges of foliage. Be imaginative: we recently attended a wedding with a seaside theme where the tables were decorated with buckets and spades filled with sand and sticks of rock with the bride and groom's names on them.

✳ Transport

There is a wide range of special transport that can be hired for a wedding, including vintage cars and horse-drawn carriages. A larger, chauffeur-driven car has the advantage of being roomy inside so the

bride can arrive at the ceremony with her dress uncreased. If spending money in this area is not one of your priorities, consider asking friends to put ribbons on their cars and to help with transport. Alternatively, if it is a sunny day and the reception is nearby, the bride and groom might like to walk, although it would be advisable to have a wet-weather contingency plan. The bride and her father generally travel from the house to the ceremony together as do the bride's mother and the bridesmaids. After the wedding, the bride and groom can leave for the reception in one car and the bride's parents and bridesmaids in the other. Whatever the arrangement, it is the responsibility of the best man to ensure that no one is left at the church and that all the guests have transport to the reception.

🎥 Video

Most of the advice on choosing a photographer also applies to choosing a company to make a video recording of your wedding. In the absence of a personal recommendation, you could contact The Association of Professional Videomakers. Alternatively, you might consider asking a friend to do the job for you, although the result will obviously be different. If you are having a professional film made, remember to discuss the choice of music that you would like on any soundtrack. If you plan to video the ceremony, remember to ask permission from the minister or registrar first.

🎥 Vows

Your vows are probably the most important promises you will ever make to another person. The making of the vows can be the most special and moving part of the day. Talk to your minister or whoever is conducting the ceremony about the wording used and make sure that you both fully understand and are happy with what you are promising. Although some couples learn their vows by heart, most take the safer option of repeating them phrase by phrase after the minister or registrar. The standard wedding vows beautifully embody all that it means to give yourselves to each other 'till death do you part'. However, if you marry in a civil ceremony, you have the opportunity to write your own vows.

🎥 Wills

The act of marriage revokes any previous will you may have made. Although possibly not top on your list of priorities at the moment, you do need to consider making new wills, or making a will for the first time. It is not the case as is generally assumed that in the event of your death everything will automatically go to your spouse and it will be easier for those left behind if they know your wishes.

TEN TIPS FOR
CUTTING COSTS

1. Weekday wedding: consider having your wedding on a weekday as venues may be cheaper. Honeymoon travel may also be cheaper midweek.

2. Dress: consider buying an end-of-line sample, buying off the internet or hiring. If you or a friend can sew well, consider making your own. Go away in your wedding clothes rather than buying new outfits. Buy or make dresses for bridesmaids that can be worn again.

3. Reception: restrict the main reception to close family and friends. Invite others to a less formal reception before or after the ceremony. Alternatively, invite them just for cake and speeches.

4. Drink: if the venue allows, bring your own wine (but check corkage charges). Serve a cheaper sparkling wine instead of champagne. Provide a paying bar for an evening reception. Alternatively, serve soft drinks only, for example, fruit punch or elderflower cordial with sparkling water.

5. Food: ask each guest to bring a dish or ask a friend to do the catering.

6. Cake: ask a friend to make it or buy it ready made from any large supermarket or store, and then ice it yourself.

7. Flowers: choose flowers that are in season (see Appendix 7). Ask a friend to arrange the flowers for you. Have a single flower (e.g. a gerbera) in a bottle on each table. Carry an informal bunch of flowers rather than a grand bouquet.

8. Transport: ask friends with suitable cars to put ribbons on them and act as chauffeurs.

9. Music: play pre-recorded CDs or tapes at the reception rather than hiring a band.

10. Photographs: ask friends to take photographs and video footage. Put disposable cameras on each table for guests to use. Alternatively, use a photographer with a smaller business who does not need to charge VAT.

PART 2

Rules

of

Engagement

WILL YOU MARRY ME?

'It's just beautiful,' she whispered, gazing down at the ring on her finger.
The diamond sparkled in the sunlight. Sarah and Jonathan were standing
on a headland overlooking the harbour. What a difference a few hours
made. She had left her small, dark, London flat that morning, glad it
was the weekend, glad that she would be seeing Jonathan again but
wondering where their relationship was heading and how long they could
maintain it at such a distance. He had met her at the station and, as
they walked to the harbour after lunch, he had proposed. It had taken
her completely by surprise. She had dreamt of that moment since she was
a little girl and now it had happened. She was going to be married and
there was a wedding to plan. Thoughts of the next few months crowded
into her head. Her train of thought was interrupted as a cloud passed
over the sun...

'Will you really love me for ever?' she said, dragging her eyes from
the ring on her left hand and looking up at him.

He paused before replying and his mind wandered back to his childhood
– the family holidays and Christmases when they were all together. He
looked away from Sarah and across the harbour to the horizon. His brow
furrowed slightly as he remembered that grey February morning when
all the colour had drained from his world. His father had spoken to him
without looking up. 'I am sorry,' he had said, 'but I need to move away.
Your mother and I are getting divorced.' He could still remember his head
reeling and the feeling of helplessness. He realized at that moment that life
would never be the same again.

He looked back at Sarah. When his parents got engaged did they
feel like this? What had gone wrong? The questions were teeming in
his brain.

'Jonathan...?' Sarah's voice brought him back to the present.

'Yes,' he stammered. 'Yes, of course I love you, Sarah. Sorry. It
just suddenly felt like a really big step that we were taking.'

We are all too familiar with the consequences of family breakdown in
our society but the good news is that most marriages last a lifetime.
However, there are probably few engaged couples who at some time
during their engagement do not step back and wonder, if only for a

moment, what the future will bring and what the secret is to being part of a marriage that lasts 'till death us do part'.

The truth is that there is no secret.

There are, however, skills you can learn, choices you can make, habits you can put in place and rules you can follow which will ensure that together you build a marriage that lasts a lifetime.

Rule 1: BUILD STRONG FOUNDATIONS

Katharine: Several years ago we spent five very wet but wonderful days in Venice. The web site that we used to book our accommodation recommended our hotel for 'location, location, location'. There was no doubt about it, we were well placed for sightseeing. However, what the wonders of technology failed to inform us was that major rebuilding work was taking place directly underneath our bedroom window.

With the exception of the pneumatic drill heralding a new day at 6.30 a.m., Richard was in paradise. Each day gave him the opportunity to study the unique methods of the Italian construction industry before moving on to enjoy the Renaissance art that was at the top of my agenda. He questioned the local residents and discovered that work on the foundations had been in progress for many months. Thousands of wooden piles were being painstakingly sunk into the mud to form a solid base upon which building could begin. We were assured that such time and effort was spent on strengthening the foundations to ensure that the building would stand the test of time and the elements.

A strong marriage needs strong foundations. There are things that we can do together to build those foundations. It will take time and effort but the result will be that we will have marriages that will stand both the test of time and external pressures.

These foundations are:

1. Building a friendship

Richard: We met at college, class R, sitting in specifically allocated seats for all lectures. Katharine was given seat 1 and I had seat 15 (directly behind seat 1). Halfway through the first term, the class went out for a meal together. Katharine has absolutely no sense of direction and, as the evening drew on, became anxious as to how she would be able to navigate her car home through the city centre. Resourceful to the end, she realized that I lived nearby and so asked if she could follow me home.

I completely mistook Katharine's intention and, on impulse, jumped out of my car at some red traffic lights, raced back to her car and invited her back for coffee.

That evening was the beginning of our building a strong friendship. Although we began to discover some of our differences, friendship was an essential part of the strong foundation for our marriage.

Friendship will continue to grow when the initial feeling of 'falling in love' has died away. Whether, like us, you have got to know each other gradually or whether you have had a whirlwind romance, a strong friendship undergirding your relationship will enable it to withstand the test of time. Building a friendship of necessity involves spending time together.

2. Spending time together

When you are engaged or newly married, you probably need no encouragement to spend time together.

Katharine: In the months before we were engaged, Richard was working in Birmingham and I lived in Bristol, so we conducted our relationship via the M5. I would leave work on a Friday on the stroke of 5.00 p.m. and travel to Birmingham. It didn't seem to matter that I spent most of the weekend either watching Richard play hockey or helping him build a kit car, as it was just being together that was important. On one occasion, I inadvertently left my bag behind and thought nothing of driving the 180-mile round trip to retrieve it the following evening, just so we could spend more time together.

In *The Marriage Book*, Nicky and Sila Lee stress the importance and value of spending time together:

> We are convinced that married couples need to continue planning special time for each other... If in marriage we continue to make time for each other, the romance will be kept alive, we shall have the chance to communicate effectively and our understanding of each other will deepen. The regularity and nature of this time together will create the fabric of our relationship over a lifetime.

Richard: Every marriage will benefit from putting this principle into practice. Katharine and I arrange to meet together at lunchtime once a week. Katharine knows that I have written this appointment into my work diary for six months ahead, and I will endeavour to schedule my work commitments around our arrangement. We have learnt to plan, to protect and to prioritize that time together, and looking back we are very glad we have. Time together will keep a relationship growing, prevent us from slipping into living parallel lives and give us a foundation upon which to build a marriage.

As well as having a weekly time together, our marriage has also benefited from planning a weekend away together once a year. We did not do this when first married and on reflection realize what we missed! Planning a weekend away becomes much more difficult if there are children but the long-term benefits it gives to the relationship far outweigh the (not inconsiderable) stress of organizing childcare.

Although time together is crucial to building a relationship, one of the tasks of engagement and early years of marriage will be learning to balance time – time together and time apart. Both are needed. Time apart (sometimes alone and sometimes with others) can cause us to value and appreciate the time we have together, so neither partner feels 'smothered'. Talk honestly together about how to achieve the right balance in your relationship.

Richard: Another practical consideration is adjusting from one diary to two. For years, we operated three diaries: my work diary, Katharine's diary and the kitchen calendar. We learnt the hard way. Years of double-bookings or committing each other to impossible arrangements has meant that we now work from one diary (the kitchen calendar). We also ensure that we regularly copy everything into our personal diaries. Find a system that works for you.

3. Recognizing your differences

Katharine: We are writing this chapter while staying in a beautiful cottage with outstanding views over Exmoor National Park. It is springtime and the field directly outside the window is full of newborn lambs taking their faltering first steps or skipping along in the spring sunshine, a reminder of new life and new beginnings.

We married in late spring and our first home together was a basement flat with a small patio courtyard. We remember our surprise a year later at the discovery of spring bulbs pushing their way through the soil in barrels outside the back door. Unknown to us, the bulbs had been lying dormant beneath the soil throughout the autumn and winter months.

The expectancy and enjoyment that heralds the arrival of spring can greet you as you begin your relationship together. It is a season of adventure and discovery. Like the bulbs under the soil, hidden aspects of each other's character may come to light but as time goes on you may not always enjoy everything you discover about each other. In the early days of marriage you may find some aspects of your fiancé(e)'s character that you initially found attractive begin to irritate you. As one man commented: 'When we were first engaged, I loved my fiancée's carefree and relaxed attitude to life. However, now we are married, I find it intensely irritating that she won't make a decision…'

After we had been married for six months, I gave Richard a card showing a man dropping his clothes onto the floor with the caption

'Dirty clothes on the floor… clean clothes in the cupboard… AMAZING!' When living with his parents, Richard's clothes seemed miraculously to find their way from bedroom floor to cupboard, being washed and ironed in transit. He had subconsciously assumed that I would adopt the same role as his mother. It took time for him to realize that he hadn't married his mother and that I had very different expectations on this issue.

We are all different. One of the challenges of engagement and the early years of marriage is to learn to work together to manage differences creatively. Far from being a negative force, our differences can complement each other and strengthen our marriage.

4. Meeting each other's needs

In order to manage your differences and to build a strong marriage, you need to try to meet each other's needs. The key to achieving this is in your attitude to each other.

Richard: No amount of comment from Katharine in those first months of marriage about the state of the bedroom floor had made any difference. It was only when I understood that, in putting the laundry into the basket, I was meeting Katharine's need for value and support that I started to change the habit of a lifetime.

Another difference that came to light shortly after we were married concerned our attitude to television. Katharine watches very little television whereas, to her great irritation, I will flick it on as soon as I come into the room. This became a source of potential conflict until Katharine realized that I watch television as a means of unwinding at the end of the day. I also then appreciated Katharine's need for the occasional television-free zone. This is an issue that occasionally still comes up for renegotiation…

Take a break

Exercises

Consider together how you will put in place strong foundations for your marriage.

1. FRIENDSHIP

Think back over the period of time that you have known each other.

Each list five things that you enjoy doing together, e.g. going to the cinema, having a meal together, walking, DIY, sport.

1..

2..

3..

4..

5..

Talk about how you can keep building your friendship when you have been married for 5, 10, 15 years.

(ADAPTED FROM THE MARRIAGE PREPARATION COURSE MANUAL, ALPHA INTERNATIONAL PUBLICATIONS)

2. SPENDING TIME TOGETHER

Think about how you can prioritize time together.

Plan a regular time when you can spend time together (doing something you both enjoy, other than planning the wedding, e.g. each Wednesday evening 8.30 p.m. – 10.30 p.m.)

This week ....

In the weeks before the wedding..

After the wedding ....

3. RECOGNIZING YOUR DIFFERENCES

Talk together about anything new you have discovered about each other.

4. MANAGING YOUR EXPECTATIONS AND MEETING NEEDS

Each consider the following statements. On a rating of 1 to 10, score how each matches your expectations (where 1 = strongly disagree and 10 = strongly agree). The object is to understand each other's expectations in these areas, many of which will be dealt with in more detail in subsequent chapters. (e.g. I expect to have the television/music on most of the time: K 2, R 8)

I expect to save money each month.

I expect to make important decisions together.

I expect a period of time on my own each day.

I expect we will go out with friends most weekends.

I expect we will share the household chores.

If we are able to conceive, I expect to have children.

I expect we will have a holiday each year.

I expect I will be relaxed if our home is untidy.

I expect only one of us will work full time.

I expect to have the television/music on most of the time.

I expect my fiancé(e) to meet my emotional needs.

I expect us both to take the initiative in lovemaking.

If either of us has a faith, I expect we will support each other in it.

I expect to see our families regularly.

I expect that we will always plan ahead.

Talk together about anything new you have discovered about each other. Think about areas where you need to change and areas where you need to accept one another's differences.

Rule 2: CHOOSE TO LOVE EACH OTHER

Tom received the following letter from his fiancée, Jo, shortly after they were engaged:

'My darling,
Thank you for agreeing to be my husband. I don't deserve you and I must be the luckiest woman in the world. I can't wait to be with you for ever. I think of you every moment of the day and dream of you at night. I will love you like this for eternity. Nothing will ever change.'

But of course ten years later things have changed. Tom and Jo remain happily married, but life has moved on for them as it will for each of us.

Being newly in love is a wonderful experience. Your emotions are heightened and you may think of each other every minute of the day and night. It is a special time and you need to enjoy it while it lasts.

However, it is important to realize that no one can live at that intensity of emotion indefinitely. Psychologists suggest that such feelings generally last about two years. After that, the nature of your love for each other will change. If your love is to deepen and grow, you must begin to use your will and not just rely on how you feel. In fact you must *choose* to love each other.

Katharine: Last week, while vacuuming the bathroom floor, I inadvertently hoovered up a sports sock that had been tossed vaguely towards the laundry basket by its owner and left to rest where it had fallen. The machine shuddered to a halt with a simultaneous emission of black smoke and a smell of burning rubber. First we took it apart ourselves to no avail. A local repairer, after a cursory glance, confirmed that it would be very difficult to fix. Resigned to further expenditure, we simply left it for disposal and purchased a new one. It was much easier to buy a new model rather than repair the old.

The sociologist, Alvin Toffler, writes that 'People today have a throwaway mentality. They not only have throwaway products but they make throwaway friends and this mentality produces throwaway marriages.' Like the vacuum cleaner, marriages are often cast aside when they no longer seem to be working.

The key to building a marriage that lasts is your attitude to the relationship. You need to choose to work at your relationship together and not simply to discard it when you hit difficult times. You need to 'begin with the end in mind' from your engagement day onwards.

Participants in a research project commissioned by Care for the Family attributed the secret of lasting marriage to the commitment they made to each other and to the marriage itself. This was described as the 'glue' of the relationship. DIY enthusiasts may be familiar with the type of glue that is bought in two separate tubes. The adhesive and the hardener need to be mixed together before being used. The two substances then work together to form a bond that cannot easily be broken. In the same way, both the public and the private work together to form the bond of marriage. Forces that are internal (your love for each other) and external (the public ceremony and status) work together to form the commitment that is the glue of the relationship.

If you are in a position to buy a house or flat together, you will need to sign a contract binding you legally to fulfil your obligation to complete the purchase. Marriage, however, is much more than a legal contract. It is based on trust and commitment between two people who are choosing to promise to love each other for a lifetime.

Whether you are planning a large, formal occasion or a small, family affair, whether your wedding is to be in a church, at the register office or another venue of your choice, the most important part of the ceremony will certainly be when you publicly make your promises to each other.

You may like to use the traditional wording:

I [Name] take you to be my husband/wife
to have and to hold
from this day forward,
for better, for worse,
for richer, for poorer,
in sickness and in health,
to love and to cherish,
till death us do part
according to God's holy law,
and this is my solemn vow.

Another way of saying this would be:

I *choose* to love you
whatever happens,
however I feel,
whoever I meet,
whenever we have problems,
whether or not I feel in love.

Steve and Jane were married in March and had planned a honeymoon in Scotland. Jane had enjoyed family holidays there as a child and was looking forward to rediscovering old haunts with Steve. They spent the first few days sightseeing and then planned to go walking in the Highlands. At the beginning of the second week when out walking, Jane found she had to stop to rest more frequently and, towards the end of the fortnight, she found she was having some difficulty breathing. She put it down to exhaustion after the stress of the wedding and tried not to dwell on it. However, a visit to the doctor on their return revealed that she had a small tumour on her lung.

Steve writes, 'When the doctor told us the news, we felt as if the bottom had fallen out of our world. I felt numb. All our hopes and plans were suddenly thrown into the air. We were faced with a very different future than that we had planned. In fact we didn't know if we had a future. A month ago I had promised to love Jane in sickness and in health. One night as I considered the prospect of the months that lay ahead I suddenly realized the enormity of what I had promised. The simple fact that we had promised to love each other whatever the circumstances was what kept us going. Our love for each other grew stronger despite her illness. Jane died two and a half years later. They were a very special two and a half years.'

Continuing to love each other is a choice. The reality is that none of us knows what the future will bring. When you promise to love your husband or wife for better or for worse, you are choosing to put their needs before yours whatever the circumstances and however you feel. You are committing yourselves to them, to seek always what is best for them. This runs counter-culture in today's 'me'-centred society but it is the only way to work together to create a marriage that lasts a lifetime.

A recent magazine article contained an interview with the actress Meryl Streep who has been married to the sculptor Don Gummer for 24 years. In the interview she expressed an unswerving commitment to her marriage and family life, despite the pressures of the world they live in. She was quoted as saying, 'Our marriage and our children and their future well-being inform all the decisions that we make.'

Just as we choose to marry each other, we also choose to stay married. 'The "till death us do part" aspect of marriage is not an untouchable ideal but a living reality that is insured by an unswerving commitment – a wilful agreement to keep love alive' (*When Bad Things Happen to Good Marriages*, Drs Les and Leslie Parrott).

Take a break

Exercises

1. Why did you decide to get married?

....

....

....

....

....

....

2. Discuss the vows you will say to each other at your wedding.

Which phrase do you find most challenging? Discuss why with your fiancé(e).

Rule 3: KEEP TALKING

Katharine: It was a Saturday in early autumn five months after we
became engaged. We had spent the day visiting a castle in Devon, and
struggled back shoe-horned into a mini with a beautiful lemon tree in
an enormous terracotta pot. During the past few months we had spent
many happy hours reading glossy magazines with full colour pages
depicting what a first home could look like. One picture that had
caught our eye was of a bare apartment that was transformed into
a dream home by strategically placed houseplants, in particular a
blossoming lemon tree.

We were thrilled with our purchase, which later took pride of place in
our first home, and lovingly cared for it, watering it daily. It flourished
and we looked forward to the harvest. Weeks and months went by and
we settled into married life. The plant got pushed behind a chair and
watered at weekends, when and if we remembered. Slowly, without
anyone noticing, the leaves began to curl at the edges, turning from
green to yellow to brown, until only the twig-like branches remained.

As one woman friend realized, looking back on her marriage: 'Our
lack of communication killed our love – it began to wither and one
day finally died – like a plant without water.'

Katharine: During my time as a family law solicitor, I saw many people
who had entered married life with the same hope, excitement and
enthusiasm with which we had bought that lemon tree, but who were
now sitting in the waiting room, facing the stark reality that their
early hopes and expectations had not been met.

*Linda was one such client. She came in, her two-year-old in a buggy,
and sat down, fighting back the tears. She told us about her marriage.
'The first couple of years of our relationship seemed great. We had fun
and were both busy with our careers. Then Amy was born and I stayed
at home to look after her. Simon was promoted and had to work long
hours. I made a life for Amy and myself at home. Simon and I didn't
have much time together and, looking back, I think we began to live*

parallel lives. I feel we don't know each other any more. We have stopped communicating about things that matter.'

Sadly, Linda's story is not unusual. Lack of communication can make two people who love and commit to each other on their wedding day eventually feel like complete strangers.

Just as the lemon tree needs water to thrive, your marriage will need good channels of communication from day one if it is to blossom and grow.

There are steps you can take to improve communication:

1. Recognize your differences

Family background

How your respective families communicated as you were growing up will have a significant impact on how you have learnt to communicate as adults. One of you may have come from a family where factual information was exchanged but feelings never openly discussed. On the other hand, your fiancé(e)'s family may be loud and gregarious, everyone and everything brought into the open, talked about and laughed or cried about.

Recognizing that your family background affects how you communicate as an adult is a vital part of learning the necessary skills to communicate with each other, especially during the early years of marriage.

Personality

Your individual personalities, whether you are natural extroverts or introverts, logical or intuitive, undoubtedly affect how you communicate.

Jon is a logical introvert and married Alex, an intuitive extrovert. Jon will think carefully about what he is going to say and his first words are usually his last on the subject. Alex, however, thinks as she speaks. She works out her opinions by talking them through. Her first words are just that and she will generally go through a raft of options before she arrives at her final conclusion. Recognizing their personality differences has helped them enormously to learn to communicate better as they start out in marriage.

2. Make connections

Richard: We had optimistically agreed to take on the task of telephoning and reserving tickets for a concert for three entire families. The booking lines opened at 8.30 a.m. on Saturday morning. At that time we would be on a train to Oxford so had put credit on the mobile phone the previous day and charged the battery overnight. Doubtless to the extreme annoyance of others travelling in the same carriage, we began ringing at 8.31 a.m. and pressed the redial button every two minutes. Each time we were greeted by the increasingly familiar and annoying pre-recorded message, assuring us that they valued our call but that all operators were busy. Finally, at 9.23 a.m., we made a connection. Credit card to hand, we set about booking the tickets and were just giving the details when the train entered a tunnel and the signal was lost. No signal, no message. Shouting louder or speaking more slowly made no difference at all. We were just steeling ourselves for the unenviable task of conveying the news to our disappointed friends when we emerged from the tunnel. Network coverage was resumed and the signal restored. By the time we reached our destination, we had made the connection, communication had taken place and we had successfully purchased the tickets.

To begin to build a lifelong marriage together, you need to learn from the outset how to be good senders and receivers of messages, making sure there is no interference with the signal. You need to learn how to express yourselves honestly and how in turn to listen, recognizing those factors that may distort the message or prevent its being heard.

It is much easier to learn such skills while engaged than several years into marriage when bad habits may have set in. There are exercises at the end of this chapter which will help you learn to talk to and listen to each other better. Ensuing discussions about how you each might feel about certain aspects of the wedding arrangements will give you much opportunity for practice!

3. Talk honestly

If you are to build a strong relationship together, you need to develop honesty in your communication and learn to talk together about how you feel. From your engagement onwards, your aim should be to move from independence to interdependence. This includes resolving to have no secrets and to share your thoughts and feelings, your hopes and your dreams. In doing this you make yourselves vulnerable. It takes courage. Be gentle with each other and go at your own pace. You have a lifetime ahead of you.

4. Listen well

We have probably all had the experience of not being listened to, of being ignored. It can make you feel angry, frustrated and insignificant. However, when someone pays you the compliment of really listening and giving you their undivided attention, the opposite can be true: you feel valued, special and loved.

Paul Tillich writes: 'The first duty of love is to listen.' Just by listening, you have the potential to make your fiancé(e) know that you love and value them. This is a skill you can learn now and continue to use once you are married. Many people are poor listeners. It is easy to slip into the habit of letting your mind wander, not really giving your partner your full attention. It is surprisingly easy to allow another agenda to run in your head or to think about what to say next while someone is speaking to you.

In order to communicate well, there are other things you need to do:

i) Be aware of your tone of voice and body language
In the film *Three Men and a Baby*, Ted Danson reads to the baby from the only literature available, a magazine on boxing. The baby is quite content because she hears merely a gentle, caring tone of voice. The content is irrelevant.

Thirty-five per cent of our communication is tone of voice. An amazing 55% is body language. Imagine one of you is upset. The question 'What's the matter now?' spoken with the emphasis on *now* and with hands on hips can have quite a different meaning from exactly the same words spoken in a gentle tone and with eye contact.

ii) Recognize interference
In the mobile phone story, the interference in the tunnel meant that no message could be communicated. No booking could be made.

Sarah and Ian have been married for five weeks. Since they got back from their honeymoon, Sarah has been very busy at work. Ian has invited some friends over for the evening. He knows that she is under pressure and wants to try to help. She knows that the last meal she cooked for his friends was a complete disaster.

He says, 'Don't worry about cooking tonight. We'll get a takeaway.'
meaning 'That will take some pressure off you.'
She hears, 'I'll get a takeaway because I don't want you to cook
another disastrous meal for my friends.'
She says, 'Don't you think I can be trusted to cook, then?'

It is easy to see how the conversation could spiral downwards unless
they are together able to recognize how the past has interfered with
the present and distorted what Sarah heard. Playing the children's
game, Chinese whispers, is fun expressly because the original message
becomes distorted as it is passed from one person to another.
However, the same distortion can occur to a message that you want
to communicate to your fiancé(e). Your separate experiences of life,
your memories and attitudes, prejudices and assumptions, can all
distort the message being conveyed. If you can learn to recognize any
distortion in the message, you can take a step back and reconnect
before any misunderstanding occurs.

iii) Choose the right time
Choose a time that suits you both.

Mike and Susannah were engaged for eight months and have recently
married. He comes to life at 10.30 p.m. at night but struggles to have
a conversation much before 9.00 a.m. in the morning. Susannah's body
clock is the reverse. They have had to work hard to find a time to talk
together when they are both at their best.
Recognizing this and each making the effort to accommodate the other
has been crucial for them in learning to communicate.

iv) Find the right place

Katharine: It can be helpful to choose not only the best time but also the
best place for you both. We know for example that it is difficult for us
to communicate when sport is on the television. So choose a physical
environment where you both find it easy to give each other undivided
attention without distraction. If necessary, turn off the television and
ignore the telephone. If you can take positive action to address this issue
now, you will be starting off your married life with good habits in place
that can be valuable for the future.

Lizzie and Jeremy have been married for five years. During the first few years of marriage, they took it in turns to cook in the evenings and ate together at the kitchen table. When their first child was born, they moved the table out of the kitchen and replaced it with a sofa so that Lizzie could sit comfortably and feed the baby. They then found it was easier to have meals sitting on the sofa, side by side, in front of the television. Three years later they have realized that the sofa has actually become a barrier to communication in their marriage. The sofa is now out and the table is back in. They have meals together at the table again, facing each other and continuing the conversations they began five years ago.

Meal times are a great opportunity to talk to each other. Eat together when you are engaged and continue the habit into marriage.

5. Understand how we communicate

Katharine: We spent the first two nights of our honeymoon in a small hotel in the Cotswolds. Our enduring memory of breakfast on the first morning was being surrounded by couples at nearby tables with the newspapers raised between them, blocking eye contact and any

conversation, other than the occasional request for more coffee and toast. We were excited about the previous day and full of memories of the wedding which we wanted to talk about. Soon we became aware that we were the only ones speaking and it felt as if our conversation was resounding around the room.

It was no effort then but the challenge is to make the effort to keep talking to each other years on into marriage (even if the sports page does look inviting).

> 'Communication is the meeting of meaning. When your meaning meets my meaning across the bridge of words, tones, acts and deeds, when understanding occurs, then we know that we have communicated.'
>
> *CHERISHABLE LOVE AND MARRIAGE*, DAVID W. AUGSBURGER

Communication is about connecting with each other. In your day-to-day relationships, you communicate with different people on different levels. When you first meet and are attracted to another person, you may begin speaking at the level of clichés and light conversation – for instance, 'How are you?' 'Fine, thanks.' As you get to know more about each other, you begin to relate more deeply. You exchange information and make stronger connections.

The diagram below shows different possible levels of communication.

Communication Ladder

A healthy, developing relationship will move up the rungs of the communication ladder. As it does so, you will share thoughts and opinions, communicate more detail about things, in the process making yourselves vulnerable to each other. Taking an interest in each other's world is the first rung of the ladder. This may mean developing an interest in a fiancé(e)'s hobby or sport, solely for the sake of sharing it with them.

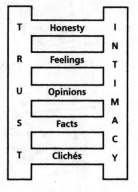

Richard: When we first got engaged, we found we did not need any encouragement to be interested in each other's lives. As well as doing things together that we both enjoyed, Katharine became an expert in building a kit car and I took a new and lively interest in art galleries.

If you can be interested in how your fiancé(e) spends the day, whether at work or at home, your friendship can be strengthened as you share the highs and lows together. The challenge is to keep being involved in each other's lives and to build new interests together. Valuing each other's beliefs and opinions, even when they are different from your own, can trigger talking about and listening to how each of you feels in a climate of total honesty.

To be able to communicate with honesty requires trust. You need to know that when you express your hopes and fears, your fiancé(e) will listen and value what you are saying and not respond with rejection or ridicule. As you climb the ladder of communication together, you will find that trust and intimacy will grow too. Moving from one rung to the next is not difficult but, as with any climb, it requires encouragement and effort. And it gets easier with practice.

Take Libby Purves' advice: 'The only real essential is to continue the conversation you started when you first met' (*Nature's Masterpiece: A Family Survival Book*, Libby Purves).

Katharine: And what about the lemon tree? It was too precious to throw away so we pruned it to get rid of the dead wood and soaked it in a bucket of water. We made time to water it regularly, gave it some sunlight and it continues to thrive...

So don't worry if your communication runs into some difficult times. Deal with the issues and your relationship will continue to grow.

Take a break

Exercises

The aim of the first exercise is to help you begin to identify and talk about how you feel.

1. Think about your wedding plans. Each write for two minutes about how you feel (e.g. I feel anxious that the wedding is only

eight weeks away and we haven't yet ordered the invitations. I feel excited about having all our family and friends together to share our day.)

Exchange the paragraphs that you have written and talk to each other about how you feel.

2. Listen/Talk

a. Choose a good time to talk when you have time to sit down together with no distractions.

b. Choose one issue to talk about. It may be something from Exercise 1 (page 71).

c. Decide who is going to speak first.

d. That person is allowed to speak without interruption for a specified period of time (if you find it helpful, the speaker could hold something in their hand as a visual reminder of whose turn it is to speak).

e. When the speaker has finished, the listener must recap what they understood the speaker to have said, including the feelings expressed. Sometimes this is called 'reflecting back' what you have heard. Then ask, 'Is that what you said?'

f. If they have got it right, the speaker will agree. If not, the speaker can have more time to explain what they mean and how they feel.

g. Speaking and repeating back can be continued until the speaker is sure the listener has understood.

h. When step (g) is complete the listener should ask whether there is anything that the speaker would like them to do to progress the matter further.

i. Now the listener in turn follows steps (d) to (h).

j. Use this structure to continue the discussion until you are both sure that you understand what the other wanted to communicate.

It may seem contrived at first but this exercise can prove a very powerful tool in helping us communicate with one another.

Rule 4: FIND JOINT SOLUTIONS

When you first meet and fall in love, you may find it difficult to imagine ever arguing.

Tom and Helen had been engaged for six months and the wedding was now only eight weeks away. They were paying for a large part of the wedding themselves and Helen was budgeting carefully, having just repaid her student loans. Tom noticed with pleasure that Helen had bought a notebook which she was using to keep account of their expenditure. Although they had agreed that they wanted a special wedding, neither wanted to begin their new life together with debts they were unable to pay. Tom considered he was lucky to be marrying someone with whom he seemed to agree on everything. As he finished addressing the last invitation, he sat back and reflected with pleasure that all seemed to be going to plan. They had booked the church and the reception. Arrangements were progressing well and so far they had kept to budget.

He was brought back from his thoughts by a ring at the door, heralding the arrival of two parcels addressed to him. He opened them eagerly. Perfect. They had arrived just in time for his stag night. He had used e-bay to source two 'Star Wars' light sabres, blue and red.

They were expensive, but he had reasoned at the time that they were just what he wanted and would provide hours of fun and entertainment. Helen came in and looked at the open parcel in disbelief. 'How much did they cost?' she asked. 'I thought we were saving money for the wedding!'

If Helen and Tom had not argued before, they now began in style. The purchase of the light sabres became the focus of a quarrel that continued well into the evening. Helen even questioned whether they should postpone the wedding.

Conflict is inevitable

Even if you are able to negotiate the minefield of wedding arrangements without disagreement, conflict is inevitably part of every marriage. We all find it difficult to set aside our own agenda and accommodate another.

Katharine: We honeymooned in Crete and thought a romantic idea would be to hire a bicycle together, side by side under a canopy, and pedal into the sunset. The only problem was that we failed to appreciate our different expectations about what a day in the saddle would be like. Richard anticipated some energetic cycling up and down the surrounding hills and set off at a blistering pace, hoping to find a secluded beach on the far side of the island.

I had an entirely different expectation: a gentle pedal along a flat terrain with time taken to enjoy the surrounding countryside. Putting my head down and cycling for the Tour de France was certainly not on my agenda, so I took my feet off the pedals and left Richard to it, simply applying the brake at necessary intervals.

We had both wanted to conduct the bike ride in the way we envisaged and neither of us made any allowance for the other which, in the heat of the midday sun, did not produce a harmonious state of affairs.

In the cool of evening, we were able to look back and reflect on the disappointment and frustration of a day which had fallen spectacularly short of our individual expectations. And the following day we resolved the issue by hiring a motorbike for the rest of the week.

Becoming engaged and then building a marriage can be like learning to share a bicycle with someone. It takes time and effort to work together and to understand each other's expectations for the journey ahead and you may at times be forgiven for wanting to pedal on your own or take your feet off the pedals altogether. The journey will certainly take you up some steep hills and over some rough terrain but, if you are prepared to find the best way forward, you can journey far.

John Gottman observes that 'Lasting marriage results from a couple's ability to resolve the conflicts that are inevitable in any relationship' (*Why Marriages Succeed or Fail*). If disagreements are inevitable in marriage, the good news is that there are steps (as outlined below) that you can learn to take to bring you together.

1. Recognize your differences

How you react to conflict depends on a number of factors, including your experiences as you were growing up and your different personalities. Understanding those differences can be the first step in helping you deal constructively with conflict when it does arise.

Family background

Recognizing how your different family backgrounds dictate your initial response to conflict is important to help you understand each other and negotiate together.

Daniel felt the colour rising on the back of his neck. He kept his eyes trained firmly on the small portion of pizza left on his plate. Carrie's parents had taken them out for a meal and it had been a perfect evening. Perfect, that is, until her father had mentioned the wedding arrangements. It seemed to him that World War III had just been declared. He dared not look up but could imagine other diners looking at their table in amazement. All three were at each other, hammer and tongs, hardly stopping to draw breath and, what was more, they almost seemed to be enjoying themselves. He couldn't remember a family argument like this at home. When his parents had a disagreement, there would be a stony silence for hours, sometimes days. But not this.

Personality

It is vital to understand that feeling anger is not wrong in itself. It is simply a sign that something is wrong. Different personalities react differently when angry. The key to resolving conflict together is to learn how to handle anger appropriately.

In *The Marriage Book*, Nicky and Sila Lee suggest that, when angry, people are likely to behave like one of two animals. You may be a thick-skinned rhino that, once angered, charges at speed, demolishing anything or anyone in its path. Or, alternatively, you may act like a hedgehog which, when threatened, curls up into a ball and sticks out its spikes. The task of marriage is to build intimacy and closeness as the years go by. It is clearly impossible to get close to a charging rhino or a prickly hedgehog.

Katharine: When we were first married, we used to think that, as only one of us behaved like a rhino when angry, only one of us had a problem. That was until one summer evening a year into marriage. It began as a trivial discussion but, as the issue widened, we both became angry and upset and I resorted to my favourite tactic of putting up an impenetrable barrier of non-communication. Richard, already annoyed because of the disagreement and faced with the frustration of a wall of silence, banged his fist hard on the bedroom door, causing substantial damage to both.

That particular evening was a catalyst for us in recognizing that internalized 'hedgehog' anger communicated by withdrawal can be just as harmful to a relationship as the 'charging rhino' approach.

We are still working at handling anger appropriately. But several years on, Richard has repaired the bedroom door.

2. Find the best time

Louise and Robert seldom argued – that is, until they got engaged. Issue after issue seemed to come between them. Disagreements over the wedding – about the timing, the music, the table plan and the budget – widened into disagreements about everyday issues that previously they had been able to agree on. Six months into marriage, Louise reflected, 'I think the pressure of the wedding arrangements caused us to argue more. It was a huge relief to go on our honeymoon and find that we could get along fine without arguing about every small detail of life.'

The times that people argue are usually those when they are most stretched. It could be just before an important occasion or when they are under pressure. Often these will be late at night. If you find yourselves engaged in a heated debate late at night, call a halt and postpone the discussion until a better time. The important thing is that the issue is deliberately deferred, not swept under the carpet or forgotten. Some friends, Pete and Nikki, told us that, having pressed the 'pause' button on a discussion that was taking place at 11.00 p.m., they set their alarm clock for 5.30 a.m. the following morning so they could attempt to resolve the issue before going to work.

Although there is almost never an easy time to resolve differences (and 5.30 a.m. may not be your preferred time to do so, particularly if you are not a 'morning person'), avoid discussions late at night. Tiredness causes issues to get out of perspective. So:

Don't try to resolve an issue late at night or just before an important occasion.

Do find the best time for both of you.

3. Don't attack each other

Jim and Pippa had agreed to open a joint account after they were engaged. Jim now looked in disbelief at the bank statement. They were overdrawn – again. He could have suggested that they methodically go through the box of receipts to see where the money has gone. Instead, he turned the attack on Pippa.

'I can't believe we are overdrawn. You are just so useless.'

A year into marriage Pippa still has an almost total recall of Jim's words and of how they made her feel.

When engaged in a heated discussion, it is important not to confuse the issue with the person. Avoid at all costs the phrases 'You always…' and 'You never…'. Instead, aim for 'I' statements to explain the issue from your perspective, for example, 'I feel really annoyed that we are overdrawn again.'

If you can learn to do this, it will explain why each of you is feeling angry and help focus on the issue between you.

4. Don't widen the issue

It is so easy in the heat of the moment to use counter-attack as a first line of defence by simply widening the issue under discussion. So 'You are so useless' is followed by 'I bet you haven't even paid the deposit for the band yet.' This is then countered with 'Anyone would think I was the only person involved in planning this wedding. I'm having to do everything. You are so selfish.' In three swift moves, the issue has widened from Pippa being overdrawn at the bank to the unrelated topic of Jim's perceived selfishness in not pulling his weight with the wedding arrangements. To resolve conflict effectively, focus on the issue rather than on attacking each other.

5. Learn the third way

After they were married, David and Jo began renovating their new property. They ripped out the fireplace which now lay in pieces in the skip and set off together to choose a new one. Four hours later, having visited every reclamation yard and grate shop in the area, they sat in a coffee shop, unable to agree. The afternoon they had been looking forward to had turned into a focus for conflict and disagreement.

Jo wanted an antique fireplace with decorated tiles. David wanted a modern one with a plain surround. Jo wanted a real fire. David wanted gas. And so on.

They found themselves getting more and more frustrated and annoyed with each other as the afternoon wore on. They sat staring into the half empty coffee cups, a wilting flower and the crumpled shopping list between them. He wished they had left the fireplace as it was. At least they agreed that they disliked it. They both felt strongly but if neither was prepared to give in, they would return home empty-handed and would have to live with a hole in the wall. Perhaps he should give in, but he couldn't bear to live with those tiles...

He took a pen from his pocket. Slowly and deliberately, he smoothed out the shopping list and began to draw. They ordered more coffee. Forty minutes later they had designed a new fireplace between them. It was completely different from either of their original ideas but they had designed it together.

Resolving conflict effectively means taking the issue that is between you and putting it right out in the open. Then together find a third way forward.

It is easy to think that when there is an issue to be resolved, it is about either winning or losing. Establishing a pattern where one of you always gets their own way and the other always gives in will not help you build a marriage where you value and respect each other. Learn to negotiate and find a third way forward on the small issues and you will know how to deal with the big issues as and when they arise. And if your first solution doesn't work, go back and try again, and again.

So Tom and Helen and the light sabres? They have resolved to use them every few weeks to remind themselves that, if handled correctly, conflict can strengthen a marriage. May the force be with them!

Take a break

Exercises

1. Talk to your fiancé(e) about how you each saw conflict resolution modelled while you were growing up.

2. What things cause you to be angry with each other?

3. How do you each react when you are angry?

4. How might you help each other react better?

5. Discuss how you could resolve conflict more constructively in the future.

Rule 5: KEEP SHORT ACCOUNTS

'... But even if we deal with conflict well there are some situations where the only solution lies a little deeper than technique...'
(THE SIXTY MINUTE MARRIAGE, ROB PARSONS)

Katharine: My parents used to live in a property with a central gutter which, during autumn and winter months, would gradually fill up with dead leaves from nearby trees. At the same time every year, Richard would receive a telephone call asking him if he would make the somewhat hazardous journey onto the roof to remove the debris from the channel.

Despite this annual expedition, we failed to learn from my parents' example. After we had married for a couple of years, we moved to a house with a flat roof. One Christmas Day, just as the turkey was ready to come out of the oven, we heard the ominous sound of running water, coming not from the bathroom but from the spare bedroom. We had failed to keep the gutter clear of leaves and inevitably a blockage had occurred, resulting in water descending through the bedroom ceiling. Seasonal festivities were put on hold whilst Richard climbed onto the roof in the torrential rain to clear the gutter (wearing swimming trunks, despite the temperature). The effect of clearing the drain was immediate. With a tremendous sucking noise, the trapped water shot down the drain and away from the house.

In the same way that a build up of leaves can cause a blockage in a gutter, a build up of misunderstanding and hurt can, over time, cause a blockage in a relationship. It is an inevitable fact of life that, intentionally or not, you will hurt each other, however much you may feel in love. If left unresolved that hurt can create a distance between you. In order to build intimacy, the hurt needs to be identified and forgiven and the channel of communication needs to be kept clear.

Some friends were recently given tips for married life at their wedding service. To their surprise, top of the list was the suggestion that they return the king-size bed to the department store. The advice was based on some words from the Bible that had been read earlier in the service: 'Don't let the sun go down while you are angry.' The reasoning given was the smaller the bed, the less chance of being able to cling on to the edge with a barrier of hurt and unforgiveness between you.

Participants in a recent survey commissioned by Care for the Family confirmed this advice. Those interviewed unanimously agreed that one of the factors that had kept their marriage going over the years was their resolve 'never to go to bed on an argument'. Accordingly, if a curfew has been called into play (see page 77) and a potentially heated discussion postponed to a better time, deal with the immediate hurt caused to each other whilst putting the issue itself on hold.

It is important to keep short accounts with each other from the very outset of your relationship. This will involve acknowledging when you have been hurt and then apologizing and forgiving.

1. Identify the hurt

Katharine: Friday night is 'family night' for us when we try to stay in and spend an evening together as a family. If the children choose what to do, the evening usually involves eating pizza and watching a video together. On one recent Friday, we visited the video shop. After lengthy negotiation and discussion, a film was selected and, armed with the statutory bag of popcorn, we queued to pay. On reaching the front of the queue we were horrified to find that a previous video we had hired was overdue. We owed four weeks of rental (a not inconsiderable sum of money). We later discovered that the video in question had been inadvertently knocked under a cushion at home and forgotten about. Had we known it was there, we could have taken action to return it immediately. However, until we spoke to the sales assistant, we had been unaware of the fact that the outstanding balance had continued to accumulate.

In the same way it is vital for each of you to begin your engagement and to build your marriage by being prepared to tell each other when there is a problem between you and when you feel hurt, so there is no possibility of building up an accumulation of grievances. This process is made much easier if you can begin by explaining how you feel, for example, 'I felt hurt when you didn't take my views into account this morning...'

2. Apologize

Once the issue has been explained it is out in the open, and the 'gutter' can be cleared, first by apologizing for any hurt caused and then by forgiving in return.

Richard: There have been many times when we have felt hurt or annoyed by something that the other has said or done. Neither of us finds it easy to admit we are wrong and to apologize as it involves swallowing our pride and choosing not to seek to justify our behaviour. However, as soon as one of us has taken the initiative and apologized, we find any irritation melts away and it is much easier to take the next step to deal with the hurt. This is to forgive.

3. Learn to forgive each other

Forgiveness is not brushing the hurt under the carpet and pretending it doesn't matter. It involves confronting the ways you may have hurt each other, bringing them out into the open and then, for the sake of the relationship, choosing to let go. Forgiveness is often costly and may require courage. Where the hurt is deep, healing may take some time.

Rob Parsons writes in *The Sixty Minute Marriage*:

'Forgiveness feels the pain but doesn't hoard it; it allows tomorrow to break free of yesterday. It is always hard, sometimes foolish and, at its heart, God-like.

There is no hope for us without it.'

The following story, adapted from *The Marriage Book*, shows how the process of apologizing and forgiving was key in enabling Deborah and Miles to deal with hurt brought with them into their marriage from just before their wedding day.

Two weeks before the wedding, Deborah went to have the final fitting for her dress. She was going from her office in a taxi at Christmas time, so London was very busy. She was in a traffic jam, feeling very excited, when she saw a couple walking away from her with their arms around each other. As the taxi drew nearer, she was shocked to see that it was her fiancé, Miles, with his arm around another woman. Moreover, she knew that the woman in question was his previous girlfriend.

Deborah said, 'It was like a horror movie. My taxi was going very slowly so I watched them for a bit longer, thinking "What shall I do? Shall I jump out of the taxi?" My heart was beating like mad. I couldn't believe my eyes. Then I saw them arrive outside her office. They said goodbye and kissed each other. It wasn't a passionate kiss, but it was enough of a kiss. At that moment my taxi picked up speed and I arrived for my fitting. I was so upset that I couldn't even cry. During the fitting I kept on asking them to hurry up. All I wanted to do was to get on the telephone.'

The truth of the situation was that Miles had been meeting his former girlfriend for lunch to apologize for his failure to end their relationship properly. As far as he was concerned, his intentions were completely honourable. He never said sorry to Deborah because he didn't feel the need to. For her the issue remained unresolved. In fact after the wedding, to add insult to injury, the story kept coming up at parties as a joke.

Several years later Miles and Deborah went on The Marriage Course (a course designed to give any married couple tools to build a healthy marriage). It was only then that they were finally able to talk honestly together about what had happened. Miles for the first time understood how Deborah had felt. He was able to apologize and Deborah was then able to forgive and, finally, let go. It was an important moment in their relationship.

To build a strong relationship together through engagement and into marriage, resolve to deal with hurt as it arises and keep short accounts with one another, first by choosing to identify and deal with hurt or misunderstanding and then by apologizing and forgiving each other on a daily basis.

Take a break

Exercise

1. Ask each other whether there is any unresolved hurt between you. (Try to explain what the hurt is and how it makes you feel.)

2. Say sorry and forgive each other.

3. Resolve to do this on a daily basis.

Rule 6: UNPACK YOUR BAGGAGE

Part One

Richard: We both have the same memories of our eighteenth birthdays. We each remember the excitement and anticipation of the large present torn open to reveal a suitcase, which was then opened to reveal another suitcase and then another, until there was a complete set. On reflection, the suitcases were perhaps a symbolic gift. At eighteen, we were free to pack our bags, leave home and move on.

One or both of you may have packed and moved on many years ago. For others, getting married will be the first time you have physically moved away from your childhood home. In either case, becoming engaged and getting married means you need to move away not only physically but also emotionally.

Whatever your situation, your engagement means that you and your fiancé(e) are setting out on a journey together. You will each begin the journey with two invisible suitcases. The first is a new suitcase, which is empty, just waiting to be packed. Together you can choose what to put in it. The second is a larger, well-worn suitcase which is already full to bursting. Packed inside is your past. Like it or not, you bring it with you into marriage. You cannot travel without it. It contains your memories, your successes and failures, the joy and the laughter, the heartache and pain that you have encountered on your journey so far.

Everyone begins engagement with a different set of luggage. As we have said, one of the tasks of marriage is to do some unpacking. It is only as you begin to understand what is in each other's suitcase that you can travel on together.

Family background

However diverse your cultural backgrounds, the influence of your parental figures and the homes you grew up in will take up a great deal of room in the suitcase. Within the context of the family, you will have observed your role models adopting methods of communication and conflict resolution, as well as demonstrating physical intimacy and forgiveness. These have moulded the preconceptions that you bring with you into marriage.

Laura and Ian called to see us six months after they were married. Ian came from a family where conflict between his parents had been loud and angry for many years. They eventually separated with some acrimony when he was a teenager. Painful years of angry words had taught Ian to avoid conflict at all costs. Laura's family had never resolved an issue without a good robust debate, but they were close to each other and loved nothing better than to get an issue out into the open. They hotly debated every matter from which colour they should paint the front door to the latest government policy on education. Laura and Ian sat at our kitchen table and showed us their wedding photographs. As the evening went on, the issue that they really wanted to talk about bubbled to the surface. Whenever a subject was disputed and Laura raised her voice, Ian's instinctive reaction was to turn and run for cover until the perceived storm had passed. This left Laura feeling hurt and rejected. She also felt a deep frustration that issues were not being resolved.

When asked how he felt when Laura raised her voice, Ian's reply was illuminating.

'I think she doesn't love me, and I am frightened that she will leave me.'

'Why do you think you feel that way?'

'I've been thinking a lot about that. I think it goes back to my parents because they shouted at each other until I was a teenager, when my Dad left. He left my Mum and he left me and I still wonder if it was my fault. Raised voices trigger memories and past hurt that I can't face so I run away to hide.'

Laura later wrote: 'In talking this issue through, we were able to unpack the way in which our backgrounds are influencing how we see things. I understand now how Ian feels when I raise my voice and I know why he reacts like he does. Just knowing this helps.'

Once you recognize past influences, you have a choice. You each have positive things from the past to value as well as negative things to be aware of. As you pack a new suitcase together, you can choose areas on which to model your relationship. Equally, you can choose the areas in which to act differently.

Family traditions

Richard: In our suitcases will also be presumptions about family occasions. The first Christmas after we were married brought to light our very different notions of what we each perceived as the correct procedure on Christmas Day. Our family traditions had differed in almost every aspect of the day: whether we attended church at midnight or in the morning, whether we opened presents before or after lunch, whether we took a hearty walk or watched television and even whether we served brandy butter or custard (we now have both!).

Roles and responsibilities

Richard: How we regard everyday roles and responsibilities around the home can also be influenced by our upbringing. Although my mother tended to clean the household's shoes, this was a responsibility assumed by Katharine's father. The result of this was dirty shoes for each of us during the early years of marriage.

In any given situation, you need to work out what is best for you and for your marriage. Unless you discuss this together, you may find that you simply take on the roles you have observed your parents or step-parents fulfilling as you grew up.

Katharine: My mother is good at map-reading and always sat in the passenger seat to map-read on family excursions. Richard's mother has never taken a driving test and his father always drove. When we were engaged, we both reverted to our parents' role. Much angst, many U-turns and one memorable trip from the Isle of Arran (off the west coast of Scotland) to Bristol (south west) via Hull (east coast) which, while providing panoramic views of the Pennines, could easily have been avoided if we had realized that for *our* marriage the best combination is for Richard to map-read while I drive. Now if Richard is driving and there is doubt over the route, he will simply pull over and, without even discussing the issue, we swap places.

Each of you has strengths and weaknesses. You need to play to your individual strengths, to pull together where you have corresponding weaknesses and work towards building an equal partnership.

While you are engaged, it is worth discussing how you think you are going to make decisions. It is obviously not practical to consult on every small detail, so agree between you which routine decisions you will each make (for example, who organizes payment of which bill) and which big decisions you need to make together.

In preparing to build your new relationship, you need to be certain that you have grasped these two key elements of marriage: first, leaving behind your parents and, secondly, uniting to begin a new life together. If you marry in church, this may be reflected in the words of the service: 'For this reason a man will leave his father and mother and be united to his wife and the two will become one flesh.'

For the sake of your marriage, it is important that you do both; that you leave and then unite, psychologically, emotionally and physically. As you begin married life, you need to relate in a new way to your parents and parental figures with whom you have had a close relationship. While you are young, you are dependent on your parents providing for your physical and emotional needs. As the years go by you learn to become increasingly independent. Your marriage signals the completion of that process. You set up home with your spouse and from then on you need to look to each other for mutual support. Naturally we value greatly our parents' continued love and support but we need to recognize that our loyalties have changed.

Richard: We were at a wedding recently where the question, 'Who gives this woman to be married to this man?', was answered by both parents together: 'We do.' It was a moving moment in the service, symbolizing the end of one stage of life and the beginning of something new.

It was their first Christmas together. All the family had been invited. Anxious to make a good impression on Nick's family, Kate had found a recipe for the Christmas pudding. The turkey had been delicious and no one seemed to have noticed that the sprouts were slightly overdone. All was going well. She felt a small sense of pride as she served the pudding. Nick's sister tasted it and confirmed that it was delicious but added, as an afterthought, that it was possibly not quite as good as the recipe her mother used to use. Left at that, the damage might have been limited. As it was, Nick readily agreed with his sister's verdict. Digging himself in deeper, he then went on to offer to obtain the recipe from his mother so Kate could make it for everyone the following year.

Not surprisingly, Kate has never made Christmas pudding since.

With the benefit of hindsight Nick realized his mistake in supporting his mother and sister in public in preference to his new wife. He later also understood how undervalued that had made her feel and vowed never to let that happen again.

This change in loyalties is likely to be as much of an adjustment for your parents as it is for you. You will also need to build a relationship with your new parents-in-law. You need to resist firmly but gently any unhelpful outside interference and establish a new independence together. While you will be grateful for your parents' advice and support, you must be sure to make your own decisions on issues that affect you both, such as where you live, what china you use or even where you hang the pictures. You can help your parents adjust to this change in loyalties by taking the initiative in maintaining contact with them and discussing issues such as the timing of family holidays, visits and phone calls.

The heated crucible of the wedding arrangements may well provide an early opportunity for negotiating with parents and future parents-in-law. The wedding itself may also provide a specific opportunity to thank your parents for all they have done for you over the years, either in a speech or perhaps in a letter. The aim of this change in dependency is to seek to build a mutually supportive relationship. In families where relationships have been difficult in the past, the marriage can herald a new beginning and may in time itself be a vehicle for healing and forgiveness.

Past relationships

You may find another significant item in your invisible suitcase that you bring with you will be the influence and memory of past relationships. Particularly if you have been married before, it is important that during engagement and the early years of marriage these issues are unpacked and recognized. Many of the issues relating to preparing for a further marriage are dealt with in the second part of this chapter.

Open your suitcases during your engagement, and continue to unpack over the years ahead. Choose together what to bring from the past and pack it in your new suitcase together.

Katharine: Our eighteenth birthday suitcases wore out last year and we threw them away. Soon we will be giving new ones to our children.

Take a break

Exercises

Try working through the following questions individually and then exchange your answers with your fiancé(e). Consider carefully what he or she has written. Then discuss the significant issues. Pay particular attention to understanding an issue that only one of you has highlighted. You may need to adjust some of your own answers as a result. In the questions we have referred to parents and parents-in-law but the exercise could equally be applied to any other significant relationship.

1. Each make a list of the four main items in your suitcase (influences from the past that you recognize you are bringing into marriage), e.g.

I never saw my parents argue and so I find conflict difficult.

My parents were physically very affectionate to each other and to us as children.

My mother died when I was 9 and I grew up with my brothers in an all-male household.

My father did all the decision making in my parents' marriage.

Discuss your lists together.

2. Does a parent (seek to) control or interfere in your decisions and the direction of your lives? If so, agree how to establish boundaries.

3. Identify any issues relating to your parents and/or parents-in-law that might lead to tension or arguments between you. How can these be resolved?

4. In what ways could you support your fiancé(e) with regard to your parents and parents-in-law?

5. How can you show your support and gratitude to your parents and parents-in-law?

6. How can you best keep in touch with your parents and parents-in-law?

7. Discuss possible Christmas and holiday arrangements.

Part Two

For those marrying for a further time the suitcase will be a little larger and may take a little more time to unpack. Whether your previous marriage ended in divorce or because of the death of your spouse, the experience of being married will not only have shaped you as a person but will also have influenced your expectations of any future marriage. At the time of engagement, past experience will complicate your emotions.

Where your previous marriage has ended in divorce

After her first marriage ended in divorce, Julie found herself amazed that someone might want to build a new relationship with her. The broken marriage had left her struggling with low self-esteem. As she later wrote, 'I knew my friendship with David had deepened, and every part of me longed for the friendship and security that he offered. However, at the back of my mind lurked fear, fear that I might be hurt again and fear of a new commitment. The last few years had been tough and I had reached the stage where I found it difficult to believe anything good could ever happen to me again.' She also found to her surprise that she had to relearn dating skills as she experienced again the wonder and excitement of beginning a new relationship.

If either partner has had a difficult relationship in the past, there may be issues of trust and commitment that surface when considering engagement and remarriage. These need to be addressed together sensitively.

Lauren's first husband's inability to tell the truth had taught her not to trust anyone again. She was now engaged to Rob and it was to be his first marriage. They both knew that if their relationship was going to grow, Lauren would need to take a risk and learn to trust again.

Rob wrote: 'I realized that I also had a part to play in helping Lauren to leave the past behind and to help her trust me. In the first months of our marriage, my work often took me away and so I would make the effort to telephone every night just to reassure her, to help her to begin to trust again.'

In order for their relationship to grow, Rob needed to recognize the issues that Lauren faced. The challenge was to be as understanding and tolerant as possible about this. On the other hand, Lauren needed to help the relationship by letting go of her past and trying to give Rob undivided attention.

If you are engaged and both of you have been married before, you need to be aware of each other's issues and to endeavour to support each other in dealing with them. This may be a long and often demanding task but one that will get easier as your relationship deepens.

Part of choosing to love our fiancé(e) will be choosing to let go of the past.

Pip had been married to Tim for two months. It was a second marriage for both of them. Pip always said that her first husband, Tony, 'had a thing about timekeeping'. Her memories of the marriage were of angry scenes if any member of the family was more than a few minutes late.

One particular evening, Pip had said she would be home by 7.30 p.m., but became stuck in a traffic jam. She had no way of contacting Tim and grew increasingly anxious as the minutes ticked by. The traffic crawled along as five minutes became ten, fifteen and then twenty. When she eventually arrived home, it was after 8.00 pm. She burst in, apologizing profusely and, without even stopping to take off her coat, began to prepare the evening meal. Tim stood by the open door, looking at her in complete astonishment.

Even though some issues from the past may surface during engagement, others may not come to the fore until the early years of marriage. The important thing is to recognize them, face them and resolve to move on together.

Eileen found that her sexual inexperience in her first marriage had damaged her self-esteem. This in turn threatened her new relationship:

'My former husband once told me I was "frigid". He had hurt me deeply at the time, but I tried to forget and bury it under the trauma of separation. I remarried several years later, and that word came back to haunt me in the context of my sexual relationship in my new marriage. The belief that my new husband too might think I was frigid troubled me greatly. It was only when I faced the issue and talked to a friend that the power that the word had over me was broken.'

If either of you has been unhappily married before, the crucial question to ask is: 'What is it about *this* relationship that means things will be different this time?' As another woman explains: 'If I had realized that I was just swapping one set of problems for another, I would have thought more carefully before getting married again. I thought the problem was my husband. I have now discovered that part of the problem lay a little closer to home.'

The truth is you must first turn the spotlight on yourselves. It is as you acknowledge what your part may have been in the breakdown of a previous relationship that you will be able to see how you can be part of building a different future.

Where you have been widowed

Becoming engaged after one is widowed, particularly if widowed young, may cause different but equally complex emotions to surface. For some, bereavement may result in a loss of confidence and reluctance to risk being hurt again. For many, the role of husband or wife will be intrinsically bound up with the person who has died. The new fiancé(e) is of course a different person and the task will be to endeavour to avoid comparisons. People need to treasure the past. Memories of the deceased are very precious and are inevitably brought into a new marriage. You should not expect a fiancé(e) to replace a spouse who has died.

A bereaved spouse considering remarriage may still have feelings of loyalty to the partner who died. One woman struggling with this issue explains: 'I felt that I was being disloyal in forming a new relationship. Talking with a friend who had been widowed herself helped me. I realized that I had promised to be faithful "till death us do part". Death had now parted us, and I was free to move on. I also knew that my husband would have wanted the best for me and deep down I knew that this was the best...'

It can be liberating to discover that you can have two wonderful marriages. You can love your fiancé(e) without in any way denying the feelings you still have for your first husband or wife.

Richard: A friend of ours who was widowed and has now remarried wrote of his experience: 'It is probably inevitable that one makes comparisons. However, they are very dangerous, both because every marriage is different and also because of the danger of hurting your partner's feelings. This is doubly so because if one's first marriage was very happy, the power of nostalgia can sometimes make it seem even better than it was. When you feel that your second marriage is not absolutely fantastic (as inevitably you will from time to time), the tendency can be to turn to overly rosy memories of your first marriage.'

Our best man married a widow who had three young children. The wedding day was very special. While not denying there was some heartache, it was a great celebration that valued the past while marking the beginning of a new future for a new family.

If you are engaged to marry someone who has been bereaved, remember that grieving does not have a clearly defined ending. Moments of grief are to be expected. These will often come without warning. Be prepared to recognize the signs and to give your partner time alone when they need it. It will be helpful also to be particularly aware of birthdays and anniversaries such as that of the date the spouse died. The most difficult and unexpected memories may be triggered by a piece of music, a fragment of verse, or even the sight of an elderly couple in each other's company. They can induce grief without warning.

Richard: Our friend's letter continued: 'The wound of bereavement cuts deep but, over time, it begins to heal. Remarriage can be part of the healing process. Whilst the scar has faded, it will never go away completely. It is thirteen years since Caroline died, and yet a couple of weeks ago I heard a piece of music that tore the scar tissue away and left me in tears. With it came the sense of disloyalty to my (new) wife, but also the comfort of a burden shared. It will probably never go away, although undoubtedly will become less a feature of life.'

If your fiancé(e) has been widowed, it is vital to grasp that it is possible for them to grieve for their first spouse while also loving you and looking forward to your marriage. The fact that they may miss their first husband or wife does not mean that they love you any less. Keep talking about how each of you feels and seek to move forward together. Talk about the spouse who has died and, particularly if there are children, listen to family memories. This will be part of moving on together and will avoid the possibility of such memories becoming taboo.

Deborah married a widower with children: 'In the early days of marriage, I did not share things I had experienced that had caused me pain as they seemed trivial in comparison with (my husband's) pain. I am sure now that it would have been better for our relationship had I done so.'

As your relationship deepens, your fiancé(e) needs the security of knowing that you are committed to building a relationship together for the future and are not seeking to bring back the past.

Practical matters

Whether you are divorced or widowed, there will be practical matters to consider in a new relationship. In marriage, the giving and receiving of a ring is a symbolic act. If you have been widowed, your first wedding ring may be very precious to you but at the same time feel very threatening to your fiancé(e). Some couples put the first ring away. Others continue to wear it but on a different hand. Be gentle and understanding with each other and ensure that you are both happy with whatever is agreed.

Many couples marrying for the first time will plan to buy or rent a property together that will be their joint new home. If either of you has been married before, the chances are that one or both of you may already have your own property and you will need to decide where you will live. Your engagement is the time to discuss practical steps that you can take to make the property feel that it is your joint home. Simple changes, such as redecorating the bedroom or putting up different pictures, may help the spouse who is moving in to feel that they belong.

Another point of concern may be photographs. Where there are children from a previous marriage, it may be appropriate to have a photograph of the absent natural parent in the children's bedroom or in albums, although probably not in the main rooms of the house.

Whatever you decide about this and other issues, the important thing is that each of you is able to talk honestly about how you feel and to move forward together, celebrating the past but not letting it cast a shadow over the present.

Where there are children

Rachel and Andrew had just arrived back from their honeymoon and eagerly opened the folder to see the photographs of their wedding day. They had both been married before and had six children between them. It had been a very special day, with both families celebrating together. However, as they looked through the photographs, it struck them that there wasn't a single photograph of them on their own. Each photograph included a picture of one or more of their six children – an indication, possibly, of the years ahead.

Where there are children involved, you will need to apply all the advice on building a relationship from other sections of this book but now it has to accommodate the children as well. Inevitably, you are taking on a complex set of relationships, often without the luxury of time and space to explore them. If you are engaged to be married and either or both of you have children, make every effort to build your friendship and guard your special time alone together.

One couple who are newly married with four teenage children find the only time they are alone together is early on Saturday morning when two children are in bed and the other two have a paper delivery round. If there are children, where possible be imaginative and seize every opportunity to be alone together.

Your engagement is the time to discuss and agree on parenting styles. Plan how you can support each other in setting boundaries and in areas of discipline. Talk through arrangements for special family occasions such as birthdays, Christmas, holidays and so on. If you can agree a way forward at an early stage, it will ensure that expectations are managed and understood.

Just as building a relationship with your fiancé(e) takes time, so does building a relationship with your stepchildren. If one of you has been used to having sole responsibility for the children, another adult joining the family will change the dynamics and require adjustment on everyone's part. When you become engaged, it is as if you open an account with your fiancé(e)'s child. The balance in the account is nil.

If the children feel resentful about the new relationship, the account quickly becomes overdrawn. You will need to make many deposits of unconditional love, care, compassion and kindness before you can begin to make any withdrawals.

A parent and child have a shared history and a strong bond between them. The task of engagement is to form a strong bond between yourself and your fiancé(e). Loving their natural parent is probably the best thing you can do for your stepchild. The weakest relationship in a new family is likely always to be that between stepchild and step-parent. They have no shared history. Their bond has to be carefully nurtured over time.

Step-parenting gives responsibility but no rights. Before committing to marriage, ensure that you have understood the full responsibility that you are taking on. If you find your fiancé(e)'s children difficult now, marriage will probably not change how you feel.

If you are engaged and marrying into a family where the natural parent has died, you might want to consider adopting the children. This will give you all the rights of a natural parent. This is obviously not a step to take without understanding its full implications. It may be something that you need to discuss with

your fiancé(e) and other family members now and return to a year or so into marriage.

However eager you are to remarry, remember that any children involved may need more time to adjust to the idea. They have not had any choice about the situation that they find themselves in and may need time for their concerns to be addressed. Take account of their needs when planning the wedding and be imaginative in involving them in arrangements. Depending on their age, they could help with decisions about flowers, the colour scheme, the music, table plan and so on. It will be an investment worth making if they can be made to feel that they are part of this new family from the beginning.

For couples marrying a second time, practising the 'rules of engagement' is complicated by the effects of the past. Keep good lines of communication open between you. Unpack and deal with the past and use it to launch your future together.

Take a break

Exercises

1. WHERE YOUR PREVIOUS MARRIAGE ENDED IN DIVORCE

i) From the list below:
Put a tick where your needs were met in your first marriage.
Put an X where your needs were not met.

Acceptance

Affection

Appreciation

Approval

Attention

Comfort

Encouragement

Respect

Security

Support

Talk about the issues raised.

ii) Each now choose three needs.

Discuss practical ways that you can meet those needs in your new marriage (e.g. I will meet your need for appreciation by remembering to thank you when you have done something for me.)

2. WHERE A PREVIOUS SPOUSE HAS DIED

i) Each write down five things you love and appreciate about your fiancé(e). Exchange lists.

ii) Use the listen/talk exercise from page 72.

If your previous spouse died, choose a particular memory from the past that impacts on the present and tell your fiancé(e) about it. In particular talk about your feelings.

If you are engaged to someone whose previous spouse died, listen and try to understand how your fiancé(e) feels.

Tell your fiancé(e) if there is anything from the past you find threatening and why.

3. PRACTICAL MATTERS

i) Identify any practical considerations you need to take into account as a consequence of one or both of you having been married before (e.g. the need to make your fiancé(e)'s property your joint home).

ii) Use the listen/talk exercise from page 72 to help you understand how you each feel.

iii) Find a joint solution (*Rule 4*), e.g. rearrange the kitchen cupboards and redecorate the bedroom or hang new pictures, chosen together.

4. WHERE THERE ARE CHILDREN

The following diagram shows different possible relationships in a new stepfamily.

David proposed to Joanna. He has two children, Laura and Annie. Joanna has two children, Guy and Sarah.

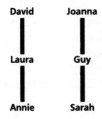 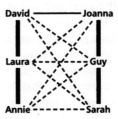

Diagram by kind permission of Christine Tufnell

Draw a similar diagram for your new family, based on the model above.

Strong bond ▮

Less strong bond ———

Weakest bonds - - - - - - -

Discuss practical ways of strengthening each of the bonds, e.g.

David ——— Joanna: We will book a babysitter on Wednesday evenings so we can spend time together.

David - - - - - - Guy: I will watch Guy play football on Saturday mornings.

Rule 7: SAY 'I LOVE YOU'

Nothing compares with the euphoria of being in love. You feel you are walking on air; you imagine that this feeling will never end. The popular music culture repeats the refrain. It is easy to say to your fiancé(e), 'I love you,' because that is how you feel.

Real love goes way beyond such feelings. It requires polishing and, like a diamond, is multifaceted and shaped over time.

In Louis de Bernières' novel, *Captain Corelli's Mandolin*, Dr Iannis describes the nature of real love to his daughter:

> 'Love is not breathlessness, it is not excitement, it is not the promulgation of promises of eternal passion, it is not the desire to mate every second minute of the day, it is not lying awake at night imagining that he is kissing every cranny of your body. No, don't blush. I am telling you some truths. That is just being "in love", which any fool can do. Love itself is what is left over when being in love has burned away… Your mother and I had it, we had roots that grew towards each other underground, and when all the pretty blossom had fallen from our branches we found that we were one tree and not two.'

Katharine: There is a cherry tree near our home. For eleven and a half months of the year, it is no different from any other cherry tree. Then in April it comes into flower: half white blossom and half pink from one trunk. Two trees have been grafted together; over the years, the two have grown as one.

Mutual attraction is usually what first brings people together. As this inevitably fades a little, there is a need to cultivate love over the years so that your roots entwine and you become one. Learning how to tell your fiancé(e) that you love them again and again in a way they understand will be part of this process.

Anna pulled the duvet tightly around her and sighed. She had just been drifting off to sleep when the noise of drilling downstairs had woken her.

They had moved into the house two months ago, just after they had returned from their honeymoon. Jon had said it would need a lot of work doing to it, but she had no idea what that really meant. A new kitchen and bathroom perhaps and a quick lick of paint. The drilling was replaced by hammer blows which pounded through her head. She hated the house: the mess, the new electrical wiring, the half-finished pipe work, the central heating still to be installed – she had never wanted to change the kitchen anyway. But more than all that, she hated them because they took him away from her.

Jon was determined to make his marriage work. He wanted to show Anna how much he loved her and wanted to provide for her by building their dream home. This would be the symbol of his undying love. Each night he would come in from work and, barely taking time to grab some food, he would give Anna a passing hug and set to, often working late into the night and over the weekend. And when a little extra cash was needed to pay for the next stage, he would show his sacrifice to Anna by staying late at work to earn the extra money needed to finish the house.

Jon was pleased with the progress he was making, two months on, still within budget and scheduled to finish by Christmas in six months' time. He stepped back to admire his progress for a moment. As usual it was a solitary experience. No Anna. Jon could not understand it; the more effort he put into their home, the more distant and remote she seemed to *become. She rarely helped and seldom showed the excitement that had been there when they first moved in.*

Richard: Last summer, I stood at the checkout of the large French hypermarket, my trolley laden with enough supplies for a school camp. There seemed to be a problem. My schoolboy French was not making any headway with an increasingly frustrated and agitated sales assistant. I resorted to speaking English to her, slowly and loudly, accompanied by some excellent and clearly understandable arm signals, but to no effect.

As the queue reached the back of the shop, Katharine returned. A quick exchange in French resulted in a transformation in the situation and in the sales assistant herself. She now graciously took payment from a card that apparently was acceptable, rather than the one I had proffered.

In order to communicate effectively, we have to speak a common language. Gary Chapman in his book, *The Five Love Languages*, lists five ways in which people communicate love to one another. These could be described as:

1. Words

2. Actions

3. Time

4. Gifts

5. Physical touch

He uses the metaphor of language to examine the different ways in which we each give and receive love. He explains that, just as we all have a mother tongue which we find easy to speak and understand, so we have a primary love language through which we understand that we are loved.

All five of these languages are important but for each of us there will be at least one in which we are fluent.

As Chapman explains: 'In order for us to feel loved by our partner, we must be "loved" in our favourite language more than any other.'

Words

Words are a powerful tool. Kind words build up; harsh words cut down and destroy. If your fiancé(e)'s primary love language is words, you can show them how much you love them simply through the words that you say. When a relationship is new, it is easy to compliment and encourage each other. The challenge is to continue that over a lifetime together.

Actions

For others, actions convey love in a very special way. The possibilities for expressing love in the language of action are endless. It could be filling the car up with petrol, organizing that surprise, going to watch your fiancé(e)'s team playing on a cold, wet afternoon or perhaps even setting aside an evening to address all the wedding invitations. Simply by performing these actions, your fiancé(e) hears that you have thought about them and care for them, and knows that you love them.

Time

If your primary love language is time, then this means time with your fiancé(e), so taking them out with a group of friends will probably not be enough. What does matter is both the quality *and* quantity of time together. It may be travelling together in the car; it may be a special date. If your love language is time, it will not matter greatly if you are both out walking and it rains, or out for a meal and the food is disappointing. It is just the single fact of being exclusively together that conveys the message that you are loved.

Gifts

Giving and receiving gifts is very important to some people. The action of procuring and presenting a gift conveys the message of love. The gift is a visual symbol; its monetary value is often less significant. If this is your fiancé(e)'s love language, a gift of a single flower or a favourite bar of chocolate can convey love in the same way as a more expensive present. The gift is a visual reminder that the giver has thought about and cares for the receiver.

Physical touch

This can be anything from brushing past each other to touch of a more intimate nature. If someone who senses love through touch receives it, they will feel all the same emotions that go with being told in words that they are loved. If that is your fiancé(e)'s language, you will need to use touch deliberately to show that you love them. As

Gary Chapman describes it: 'To touch my body is to touch me. To withdraw from my body is to distance yourself from me.'

You need to make the effort to learn to say 'I love you' to your fiancé(e) in a language that they can understand. Just as in the French supermarket, the effects can be far-reaching. In fact, what often happens is that you try to communicate love to your fiancé(e) in the way *you* understand it. However, if this is not their primary love language, it will be like speaking a foreign language to them.

Jon was working supremely hard to build a home for Anna. Every hole drilled and hammer blow said 'I love you' but it was falling on deaf ears. Anna's language was time – time together.

Katharine: When we were first married, I would scour the shops for a birthday present for Richard, or occasionally buy him a present for no apparent reason other than to say 'I love you'. I was repeatedly disappointed when the gift was opened and simply put to one side with, at best, a grunt of thanks. Conversely, Richard's apparent incapacity to commit any time to shopping when my birthday or Christmas was on the horizon would also give me the impression that Richard did not love me.

One of Richard's primary ways of feeling and expressing love is through action. On many occasions he has spent hours tidying the house and then felt disappointed when I have sailed in, apparently oblivious to the transformation. He also loves arranging surprises. During our engagement and first years of marriage, he went to great effort to arrange many (beginning with the honeymoon) as a way of showing his love. It was not until several years later that I told Richard just how much I hate surprises. All his effort had completely missed the mark.

Over the years, understanding our differences and learning to show our love in a different language has transformed our relationship and enabled us to say 'I love you' in a way that we each hear and understand. On a good day, I receive the flowers and Richard the surprises.

When Jon and Anna heard about the concept of love languages, Jon said: 'It was like a light coming on. I suddenly grasped what was happening in our relationship. The hours I was spending on the house meant far less to Anna than they did to me. In fact, the investment of time in the building was having a negative effect because I discovered that Anna's primary way of feeling loved was through the time I spent with her, not the time I spent on the house. I was saying "I love you" through the action of building a home; what Anna wanted from me was some of that same time. I am now trying to give Anna the time that she needs.'

Anna said: 'I understood for the first time that Jon was saying he loved me by spending time on the house. I had only heard he loved the house more than me. It made sense of all the work and effort he was putting in, so I have had to learn to adjust and do some of the work with him. Jon then feels loved by me as I speak his language, and in that way I also get some extra time with him.'

Just as it takes years for the roots to entwine and for two trees to become one, so learning each other's love language and putting it into practice takes time and effort. It is an investment, however, that will realize a return that will last a lifetime.

Take a break

Exercises

Write down up to six occasions when you have been especially aware of your fiancé(e)'s love for you, e.g.

1. I know you love me when you come to watch me play football.

2. I know you love me when we go out for coffee together.

Then write down up to six occasions when you believe you have shown your fiancé(e) that you love them, e.g.

1. I have shown you that I loved you by cooking a meal for you.

2. I have shown you that I loved you by putting my arm around you at the cinema.

Taking into account what you have written, try to put the five languages of love in order of importance for you, assigning the most important to number 1. Then write down the list for your fiancé(e). When you have finished, compare what each of you has written. Resolve to use your fiancé(e)'s top two love languages this week.

ADAPTED FROM *THE MARRIAGE PREPARATION COURSE MANUAL* (ALPHA INTERNATIONAL)

Rule 8: DEVELOP INTIMACY

Richard: I took the tin out of the oven and looked in disbelief at the flat pancake that I had intended to serve with the joint. The recipe had said plain flour but there was none in the cupboard. I had substituted self-raising flour instead, reasoning that it would result in a slightly more elevated Yorkshire pudding which would be sure to impress...

In every recipe there are certain ingredients that must be included to ensure culinary success. The same principle can be applied to a marriage. Your relationship will not stand or fall on the quality or quantity of its lovemaking alone, but developing a fulfilling sexual relationship is an important part of a successful marriage. Nicky and Sila Lee write: 'Both need to recognize that their sexual relationship is not the icing on the cake of their marriage but an essential ingredient of the cake itself.'

As already discussed, the task of engagement is to prepare for a relationship of growing intimacy as you share your life together. Just as in other areas of your relationship, there are things you can learn which will help you develop intimacy in the way that you communicate and relate to each other physically. As one man said: 'I imagined that when we were married we would make love every night, and didn't think that there was much to learn. We now realize to enjoy sex we need to work at it, as with every other area of our marriage.'

This very intimate act of making love requires you to be completely vulnerable with each other in a place of safety, trust and honesty.

In marriage you promise to give yourselves unreservedly to each other and it is that commitment that forms the foundation of the marriage relationship. Giving yourselves to each other as you make love together, within the safety of the marriage vows, can be seen as the natural carrying out of that commitment.

Developing a sexual relationship should be one of the most pleasurable tasks of marriage which can continue well past child-bearing years.

'In a good marriage, sex and love are inseparable. Sex serves a very serious function in maintaining both the quality and stability of the relationship, replenishing emotional reserves and strengthening the marital bond' (*The Good Marriage*, Judith Wallerstein).

The consequences of making love go far beyond the moment. Each time you make love together, your marriage is strengthened. While one purpose of sex is obviously to have children, sex is also for your enjoyment throughout your married life together. It will be no surprise to realize that in this area, as in every other, people come to engagement with different experiences and attitudes. The following might influence your expectations of your sexual relationship.

Family background

Your expectations will be moulded partly by the attitude to sex and physical intimacy that you saw modelled as you were growing up. Recognizing these influences on you will give you a starting point for working at your relationship together.

Hannah went to boarding school when she was eleven. Although she knew that her parents loved her, they did not show their affection for her physically. She reached adulthood believing that sex was a taboo subject and an optional extra in a relationship. Her inhibitions were deepened by an incident in her teens that left her frightened of physical intimacy. Her fiancé persuaded her to seek counselling and, helped by his patience and gentleness, they were able to begin to build a fulfilling sexual relationship in their marriage.

It's always absolutely fabulous

Sex in the media is nearly always portrayed as absolutely fabulous and divorced from any committed and long-term relationship. As you prepare for marriage, you would do well to understand that, even though the sexual relationship is indeed an integral part of the marriage relationship, it is unlikely to be always absolutely fabulous.

In *The Sixty Minute Marriage*, Rob Parsons writes:

'If we are going to have a good sexual relationship, one of the prerequisites is that we stop taking ourselves so seriously and quit imagining that our sex lives are going to impress Hollywood. In that particular suburb of Los Angeles, it seems that the sex is always wonderful. The beds are always made, the women look fantastic and seem to have an insatiable appetite for lovemaking. The men are animal-like and yet tender, rough yet smooth, and never fall asleep straight afterwards. The real world is a little different. In the real world, there are periods and mind-numbing tiredness. Enjoy the films but don't compare your love life to them.'

Knowing your differences

Just as you need to understand the expectations that you bring with you, you also need to come to marriage aware of the differences between you and your fiancé(e).

It is generally held that men and women are different from each other in their approach to sex. In *The Marriage Book*, Nicky and Sila Lee write:

'Men can't get enough sex; women can't get enough romance. Men are thinking about the destination; women are thinking about the road. Men are like gas cookers: they heat up instantly and cool down rapidly. Women are like electric cookers: they take time to heat up but stay hot much longer.'

Such generalizations are just that – they do not apply to every man and every woman. It is important to interpret them for your own relationship. However, it is not uncommon for one partner to be more interested in sex and more easily aroused than the other. The key is to understand your sexual differences as individuals. The following may help (but be wary of generalizations).

Understanding what arouses you

In most cases, arousal is more complex for a woman than for a man. For many women, their attitude to sexual intercourse is inextricably linked with the quality of the relationship as a whole. To be able to give herself intimately to her husband, a woman usually needs to feel valued and secure.

Rob Parsons writes in his book, *Loving Against the Odds*:

'A wife wants to know that she is wanted – not just for sex but to talk with; loved enough to be the recipient of displays of affection which are unrelated to sexual intercourse – and loved enough to be wooed. If a man is uncommunicative and is more interested in the sports page than discussing issues that matter to her, then he had better take the sports page to bed – he's going to have plenty of time to read it. That's why the old advice is true: "If a man wants a wild Friday night, he had better begin working on it Monday morning…"'

It is as a husband meets his wife's emotional needs that he will create the climate of trust for her to be able to give herself to him. Walter Trobisch puts it like this: 'A woman's greatest erogenous zone is her heart. And nothing touches her heart more than loving, affirming words.'

On the other hand, arousal for men is often less complex and more immediate. Men can be aroused simply by the physical proximity of their partner. A conversation in the film, *The Story of Us*, comments on the perceived differences between men and women: 'After an argument, men need to make love in order to make up, whereas women need to make up before making love.'

Whatever our differences, it is vital that we communicate about this deeply intimate area of our relationship.

Knowing the importance of romance

Romance may be more important to one of you than the other. Often, romance plays a significant part in lovemaking for women. You need to take time to find out what things your fiancé(e) finds romantic. Romance can draw us together and give us feelings of closeness, intimacy and security. It can alleviate the routine of work and chores, paying bills and solving problems. Romantic acts need not incur great cost. They may simply involve doing something that is outside routine and which may require a little care and planning.

Planning ahead

As you learn about each other, you can discover how to unlock the pleasures of physical and emotional union. Each of you should take some responsibility for your part in that.

Cathy has been married to Greg for nine months. She says: 'Despite my high expectations, our sexual relationship didn't get off to a very good start. We both had demanding jobs and evening commitments and so didn't get to bed until late, by which time I just wanted to go to sleep. I never initiated lovemaking because I assumed that should be the man's role.'

Greg continues: 'Being married was great, but my one disappointment was with our lovemaking. Cathy would turn over and go straight to sleep and I would be left feeling frustrated. One evening, we met up with a couple from our marriage preparation course. It was so good to be able to talk about how I felt. As a result, we resolved to plan times to make love and Cathy agreed to take some responsibility for taking the initiative. We are still working at it but it is no longer the source of hurt and frustration that it was rapidly becoming.'

Cathy agrees: 'It was good to be able to talk and for me to realize just how Greg felt. I also found it helpful to realize that I had an important part to play. I could choose to take the initiative in our lovemaking, and that choice could override feelings of tiredness. We still have a long way to go but that evening was a real breakthrough.'

Although planning a time to make love may sound clinical, it does not rule out spontaneity as well and does ensure that this important part of your relationship does not become the casualty of your busy lives. Future circumstances, such as the birth of children or stress at work, may mean that either one of you may lose your desire for lovemaking for a period of time. When this happens, as it surely will, keep an open channel of communication about how each of you feels so as to prevent hurt and misunderstanding.

It is important to begin to communicate about your physical relationship while you are engaged and to agree any boundaries that you may wish to put in place.

Putting the past behind you

Your sexual relationship can only develop and grow in a climate of trust and honesty. You may come to marriage with previous experiences of sexual relationships. It is important that while you are engaged you bring into the open and deal with any issues that could cause guilt, jealousy or mistrust so that they do not cast a shadow over the present.

Judy had been in previous long term relationships before she met Steve.

Steve explains: 'When we got engaged we wanted to make a new start together. I knew that Judy had had sexual experiences in the past and I was worried that she would always be making comparisons with me. I didn't know how to bring the subject up.'

Judy continues: 'I knew this was an issue we needed to talk about, but I didn't know how. I was worried that when Steve knew all about my past he might think that I wasn't good enough for him. A friend recommended that we did a marriage preparation course which involved completing a questionnaire and using it as a basis for discussion with another couple about our expectations of marriage. It was such a relief when the subject of sex came up. It was quite hard to talk about it but we were both able to say how we felt and to explain our hopes and fears. Just being open with Steve about the past was very healing. We have dealt with it now and have resolved to move on. I have also thrown away my box of photographs and letters so we can really make a new start.'

Being open with each other

If either of you have issues from the past relating to matters such as pornography, abortion or sexual abuse, it would be advisable to seek outside help during your engagement so that these issues can begin to be addressed. Working through the past can be painful but it has been demonstrated that marriage can be a vehicle for healing, forgiveness and a new start.

A person's sexuality is a deeply personal part of their life. You may initially find it difficult and embarrassing to talk openly about it to each other. Do persevere. It is much easier to develop a fulfilling sex life if you are able to talk together about what each of you finds pleasurable. You may find it helpful to read a good book about sex together (e.g. *The Relate Guide to Sex* by Sarah Litvinoff; *Intended for Pleasure* by Ed and Gaye Wheat; *The Gift of Sex* by Clifford and Joyce Penner) and to use it as a basis for discussion during your engagement.

Children

A possible outcome of marriage that it is vital to discuss during your engagement is whether or not you plan to have children and how you each might feel if that were not possible.

Maria looked back on her marriage to Carl. 'Carl had been married before and had children from his previous marriage. He told me that he didn't want any more children, but I thought that once we were married I would be able to persuade him to change his mind. It's hard letting go of your dreams.'

If you have not done so already, and it is appropriate, it is also important to discuss and agree on methods of contraception.

Honeymoon expectations

Katharine: On our honeymoon, we spent the first two nights in the Cotswolds and then went to Crete. Here, the hotel rooms were individual small stone buildings set amid beautiful gardens.

We arrived in the early afternoon and carried our cases (still dropping confetti) through an avenue of bougainvillea to our room. It was a beautiful setting and the sea was glistening in the distance beyond. All was going to plan.

Other couples had told us not to expect too much. But this was our honeymoon and we knew our experience would be different. Two minutes later reality crashed in upon us as we stood on the threshold open-mouthed at the sight of two rock-hard single beds, each built into the stone wall and at least ten metres apart!

Although for some lovemaking on the honeymoon is wonderful, it is certainly not unusual to experience difficulty and for initial expectations not to be met.

Phil pushed out the boat and booked a five star country hotel. They had planned the rest of the honeymoon together but the first night had been his responsibility alone. They arrived at the hotel tired and much later than anticipated but flowers and champagne were waiting for them in their room. Jenny was delighted. They opened the champagne and talked about the day. Phil then went to shower, leaving Jenny to relax. Twenty minutes later he came out of the bathroom to find Jenny, lying across the bed – fast asleep. He decided not to wake her but nonetheless spent the rest of the night hugely disappointed. He had put so much effort into planning everything and felt badly let down. Although things improved slightly during the fortnight, both agreed that lovemaking on their honeymoon never reached the heights of passion that they had anticipated.

Have realistic expectations of lovemaking on your honeymoon and talk about them to each other. You will have had a wonderful but exhausting day and your wedding night may not be the best time to anticipate a great sexual experience. You have a lifetime ahead of you to develop a sexual relationship that deepens in intimacy over the years.

Take a break

Exercise

Read the following statements on your own and then use them as a basis for discussion. Persevere even if you find it embarrassing. Honest discussion will give you a basis for a fulfilling sexual relationship. What do you believe?

Real intimacy can only be expressed through sexual intercourse.

The husband should take the lead in lovemaking.

The husband should be the one most knowledgeable about sex.

Lovemaking is for the bedroom – under the duvet with the lights off.

Lovemaking is only for last thing at night.

Contraception should be the wife's responsibility.

One partner should never deny the other.

'Sexy' nightwear is important.

A couple must always agree their form of sexual activity.

An orgasm must be achieved for sex to be successful.

Tenderness is more important than technique.

Sex should not be practised when the wife is having a period or is pregnant.

There are no bounds to sexual activity within marriage.

(ADAPTED FROM *LOVING AGAINST THE ODDS*)

Rule 9: SPEND WHAT YOU CAN AFFORD

Leyla got in from work before Phil that evening. As she put the kettle on, the phone rang. The brief conversation that followed left her head spinning.

'Can I speak to Mr West please?'

'No, sorry. He won't be in for another half an hour. This is his wife. Can I ask who's calling?'

'The bank.'

Leyla's heart sank.

She and Phil had taken out a credit card just before they were married to pay for their contribution to the wedding. They had kept good account of expenditure at the time and were paying off the debt at an agreed monthly rate. However, two months ago, Phil's parents had come for the weekend. Leyla had wanted to make a good impression so she had bought extras in the weekly shop that she knew they couldn't afford. In the supermarket queue, she had looked at the trolley and decided on impulse to use the credit card. Phil would never notice. That had been the beginning. Over the next few weeks, she had slipped other items on the card that she needed – some new clothes for work, a birthday present for Phil, another supermarket shop. Using a plastic card didn't feel like she was spending real money and, as long as she got to the post before he did in the morning, he would never know...

Every day letters arrive offering more and more credit to 'take the waiting out of wanting'. Finance lenders come in all shapes and sizes and are now prepared to offer sums several times higher than a couple's income. Some even allow self-certification of earnings and there is no longer any requirement to demonstrate a regular pattern of saving. This has opened wide the door of opportunity for newly married couples to purchase a home. At the same time, it has greatly increased the pressure of debt. Borrow money, but borrow wisely and for items that you need – a house to live in, or a car to get to work – not just to boost your standard of living.

Katharine: During my time as a family law solicitor, conflict over finance figured high on the list of reasons cited as contributing to the breakdown of marriage. I learnt then that debt is no respecter of person, status or income. Whatever you are earning, the temptation is always to spend that little bit more than you can afford. We live in a society that pushes the use of credit but offers little guidance in managing debt. It is unfortunately often true that the more people earn, the larger their debt.

The casualties of debt sat in the waiting room outside my office. The director of the pharmaceutical company, the newly qualified surveyor and the check-out assistant experienced at first hand the crushing worry that debt can bring and the fatal blow that it can deal relationships if not handled properly. Each had used money foolishly and then, feeling the weight of guilt, had retreated behind a wall of silence and secrecy which ultimately proved too hard to scale.

Healthy marriages that last a lifetime need trust and honesty. This is just as important in the area of finance as it is elsewhere in the marriage.

Family background

In the management of money, as in other areas, you need to begin your engagement by understanding your differences and sharing your financial expectations. It will be the attitude to money, and not the relative standard of living in the homes you have been brought up in, which will have influenced how you manage your finances.

Richard: Our respective families have very different levels of income but both are generous and both have always lived well within their means. Nonetheless, although we did not have excessive debts, our different backgrounds did mean that we brought into marriage different spending priorities which we needed to reconcile. In the early days of marriage, we often had differences of opinion over our individual classification of 'essential' and 'luxury' items. Discussions frequently centred on the contents of the supermarket trolley, the focus of debate being the purchase of items such as fresh orange juice and ground coffee.

When you are engaged, you need to recognize and understand the different attitudes to money that you are each bringing into marriage from your family backgrounds.

Personality

Some people get pleasure out of spending their money and others get enjoyment out of saving and seeing their reserves grow. As in every other area, the important thing is to recognize your differences and plan your approach to money together accordingly. If you don't already know, you need to discover if you are marrying a spender or a saver.

Spender/Saver Test

1. Do you know exactly how much is in your bank account at any given time?

2. Do you have a regular pattern of saving?

3. Do you generally compare prices before buying?

4. If you are employed, do you have any of your pay left by the time your next pay cheque arrives?

5. Do you only buy essential items?

If you have answered 'Yes' to most of these questions, you are probably a saver.

If a spender marries a saver, there is obvious potential for conflict. However, when budgeting, it is an advantage to have both character traits represented. The challenge throughout marriage is not to allow conflict over money to become an issue between you. Whatever your personality, communication is critical.

Katharine: We remember one occasion when we had a sum of money in a joint savings account. One Saturday afternoon, we were shopping separately and failed to discuss our intentions in any detail. Between 2.05 p.m. and 2.30 p.m., we each independently spent the (not inconsiderable) sum of money on entirely different items in different shops. Not only did we have to negotiate with each other but also with the bank as to the terms of repayment.

Managing your money together

Whatever the exact wording of your wedding vows, it is likely that you will promise to share all you have with your fiancé(e).

Richard: The promise we made to each other was: 'All that I am I give to you, and all that I have I share with you, within the love of God.'

The fact that we share everything is the starting point when we discuss together how we manage our money. When we were engaged, opening a joint bank account seemed to us a natural way of expressing the fact that we were moving from two separate lives to one joint one. I made the appropriate arrangements at the bank but three months into marriage was perplexed to find that the account seemed to be permanently overdrawn. Further investigation resolved the mystery. It transpired that only one of us had got round to arranging to pay our salary into the account. After more discussion, we both agreed to pay a proportion of our salaries into the joint account with an agreed amount being left for us to save or spend individually.

Our financial circumstances have changed more than once over the years. While we were training, we managed with very little money. After a few years of marriage, we both qualified as solicitors and moved from a flat to a house. Our standard of living rose substantially. Then, it seemed overnight, things changed again. Our first child was born. Katharine stopped work and I took a planned year out of law with a corresponding cut in salary. During that time, although we had to curb our expenditure, it is true to say we were no less happy than when we were living off two incomes.

Once you have decided whether you are a spender or a saver, agree how much, if any, money you intend to give to charity. If you share the same beliefs and value system, this may not be difficult. However, if you differ in your approach, learn to respect each other's views and to agree a way forward that you are both happy with.

Working out a budget

The very process of working out a budget together has a number of benefits. In particular, it will give you a clear picture of your joint financial position and be a catalyst for frank discussion.

It is recommended that you open a joint account. This reflects the fact that everything you have is shared. Agree an amount you are happy for each of you to spend individually without consulting the other.

Whatever your financial situation, the following steps will help you communicate about your finances from day one and prevent money becoming a source of tension between you.

While you are engaged, discuss:

1. your individual financial positions. If you are in debt, agree your plans for repayment

2. whether you will have a joint account/separate accounts/both

3. how much each of you may spend without consulting the other

4. who will manage your finances – husband/wife/jointly

After you are married:

1. Complete the spreadsheet at the end of this chapter. This will help you see exactly what money you have available and what your known future expenditure will be.

2. If your expenditure exceeds your income, the solution usually is to reduce your expenditure. First, check that you are claiming all benefits to which you are entitled. Then define essentials and luxuries. Cut down on luxuries until the figures balance.

3. Set aside a regular time each week to review your financial position. Go through bank statements, bills, cheque book stubs and debit receipts until you have an accurate picture.

Finally, if you find managing money difficult:

1. Buy a notebook and write down all the money you spend (include everything).

2. Cut up your credit card.

3. Go back to using cash.

4. Seek further help if you need it, for example from Credit Action, a national money education charity (helpline telephone: 0800 591084, web site: www.creditaction.com); independent financial advisers; debt counselling agencies; or a friend you know and trust.

Budgeting for the wedding

This is dealt with in detail in the first part of this book (page 20). Whatever the arrangements for paying for the wedding, financial decisions will need to be taken. Working to a budget with your fiancé(e) will be good practice for budgeting together in your married life.

Income and expenditure calculator

Income (monthly) £

Salary/pay (including overtime)	....
Tax credits	....
Income support	....
Child benefit	....
Maintenance/CSA	....
Housing benefit	....
Council tax benefit	....
Disability benefit	....
Other benefits	....
Other income (e.g. return on investments)	....

Income total   £.........

Expenditure 1: Formal commitments (monthly)   £

Mortgage	....
Rent	....
Council tax	....
Maintenance	....
Water rates	....
Sewage rates	....
Electricity	....
Gas	....
Oil	....
Coal	....
Telephone	....
TV licence	....
Car MOT	....
Car loans	....
Car tax	....
Car insurance	....
Personal insurance	....
Private pension	....
House/house contents insurance	....
Personal loan repayments	....
Credit card repayments	....
Charity	....
Catalogues	....

Expenditure 1 total   £.........

Expenditure 2:
Regular spending   £
(multiply to monthly)

Food	....
Petrol	....
Public transport	....
TV/video player rental	....
Entertainment	....
Drink	....
Pets	....
Launderette	....
Children's pocket money	....
Childminder/babysitter	....
School lunches	....
Chemist	....
Cigarettes	....

Expenditure 2 total   £.........

Expenditure 3:
Occasional costs   £
(divide to monthly)

Christmas	....
Clothing	....
Holiday	....
House repairs	....
Car repairs	....
Veterinary bills	....
Redecoration	....
Birthdays	....
Optician	....
Dentist	....
Travel	....
Replacing household goods (e.g. washing machine, furniture)	....

Expenditure 3 total   £.........

TOTAL MONTHLY EXPENDITURE

Total 1 + Total 2 + Total 3
Grand total   £.........

BALANCE

Total income   £.........

Total expenditure   £.........

Monthly surplus/ shortfall   £.........

ADAPTED FROM *A FAMILY'S GUIDE TO BETTER MONEY MANAGEMENT* (CREDIT ACTION)

Rule 10: KEEP ON BUILDING

Richard: We have a colourful and somewhat eccentric friend called Jim who calls round to mow our lawn in exchange for sandwiches, telephone usage and various other small favours. Jim's favourite occupation in life is making a bonfire and he can make a bonfire unlike any other. On 5 November, our attempts usually only result in clouds of smoke which eventually peter out and serve only to upset the neighbours. On one occasion, in desperation, we doused the bonfire with a can of petrol and stood back as the flames leapt up impressively, only to see them die away in minutes.

Jim's bonfires, by contrast, last for days. One day, when asked the secret, his reply was simple: 'Build a good base and keep it well fuelled.'

You would do well to take this lesson on board in your marriage. Build a good base: use your engagement to prepare not only for the wedding day but also for the years ahead. Work through the exercises in this book together. Consider taking part in a marriage preparation course and learn effective skills to help you build your relationship. (For details of a marriage preparation course in your area, contact The National Couple Support Network, NCSN@cff.org.uk)

Then keep your marriage fuelled. Use the skills on a daily basis. Spend time together, have fun together and learn to say 'I love you' again and again.

Katharine: Last week one of our children gave us a wedding anniversary card. The message inside read: 'Mum and Dad. Congratulations on your wedding anniversary. Keep it up!' Good advice indeed from an 11-year-old.

If you have considered attending a marriage preparation course, you may have been offered a link with a support couple who can act as mentors as you begin this adventure together. If not, consider finding a couple you know who have been married for at least five years and ask if both of you can meet with them from time to time to talk to them about their experience of the ups and downs of married life.

Two years into marriage, consider working through a course, such as Connect2 or The Marriage Course, in order to refresh and refuel your relationship.

Richard and Katharine: James Jones, now Bishop of Liverpool, gave us a valuable piece of advice at our wedding: 'A marriage that works is a marriage that works for others.' We have found that to be true. There have been seasons when we felt that it was as much as we could do to keep our heads above water. However, what has strengthened our marriage more than we could have ever hoped or imagined is when we have been able to look beyond our own needs and to reach out together to help others.

A bonfire, built on a solid base and kept well fuelled, will keep burning in the rain, wind and snow and will be a source of warmth and hope for any who gather round it.

'It's just beautiful,' she whispered, gazing down at the ring on her finger. The emeralds on the eternity ring sparkled in the sunlight. Sarah and Jonathan were standing on the headland overlooking the harbour, watching their grandchildren throwing stones into the water below.

Sarah thought back to how they had stood on this headland thirty years ago, just after Jonathan had proposed. The landscape had looked quite different then. New developments had sprung up and the harbour was busier. The years had changed them both as well. 'For better, for worse' – those were the words that had kept them going through the tough times and the plain sailing. What would the next thirty years bring? Sarah looked up at Jonathan. He took her hand. 'I love you, Sarah,' he said...

APPENDICES

1 Are You Ready for Marriage?

It is not unusual at some time during your engagement to wonder, if only for a moment, whether you are making the right decision. However, if serious doubts persist, we recommend that you talk honestly to someone you know well and respect.

It takes great courage to postpone a wedding or even break off an engagement but, however hard, it is much easier to take action now than to live with a decision that you later regret.

In any event, you may find it helpful to answer the following questions individually.

The sharing test
Do I want to share the rest of my life with my fiancé(e)?

The strength test
Does our love give me energy and strength or does it drain me?

The respect test
Do I respect my fiancé(e)?

The habit test
Do I accept my fiancé(e) as they are now (bad habits and all)?

The quarrel test
Are we able to admit our mistakes, apologize and forgive each other?

The interest test
Do we have interests in common as a foundation for friendship?

The time test
Have we weathered all the seasons and a variety of situations together?

If you are unable to answer 'yes' to the questions above, we suggest you discuss your feelings with someone other than your fiancé(e).

FROM *THE MARRIAGE PREPARATION COURSE MANUAL* (ALPHA INTERNATIONAL), ADAPTED FROM *I MARRIED YOU* BY WALTER TROBISCH (IVP 1973)

2 Suggested Wording for Newspaper Announcement

National newspaper

The engagement is announced between Richard, only son of Mr and Mrs William Cox of Maidstone, Kent, and Helen Jane, youngest daughter of Mr and Mrs George Brown of Bath, North Somerset.

Local newspaper

Mr and Mrs George Brown of 32 Berkeley Road, Bath, North Somerset, are pleased to announce the engagement of their daughter, Helen, to Richard, son of Mr and Mrs William Cox of Maidstone, Kent.

3 Wedding Invitations

The style and wording of the wedding invitation will be governed both by the style of the wedding and by your personal taste.

Formal invitation

A formal invitation is generally engraved in black or printed on folded white paper. The name of the guest is handwritten in the top left-hand corner.

The traditional wording for a formal wedding invitation is as follows:

Mr and Mrs James Brown
request the pleasure of your company
at the marriage of their daughter

Rachel

to

Mr Steven Williams
at Christ Church, Compton,
on Saturday 27th April
at 2.30 pm
and afterwards at
Leighton Hall

RSVP
12 HARLEY PLACE
HEYWORTH
NORTH SOMERSET

Alternatively, the invitation can be set out as follows, leaving a space for the name of the guest in the body of the invitation:

Mr and Mrs Brian Stevens
request the pleasure of the company of

at the marriage of their daughter Ella
to
Mr Simon David Jenkins
at St Mary's Church, Westhampton,
on Saturday 6th December
at 12 noon
and afterwards at the Grange Hotel.

63 Westhampton Road
Selbeigh
North Yorkshire
NY22 3PR

RSVP

The same wording can be used for a civil ceremony.

Individual family circumstances need to be reflected in the wording of the invitation. The basic guideline is that the host or hostess sends the invitation and their relationship to the bride should be made clear.

Traditional alternative wording to suit different family circumstances is set out below. However, there is no hard and fast rule, and the suggestions below are proposed as a guide only.

When the bride's mother is host:
Mrs Rosemary James requests the pleasure of your company at the marriage of her daughter…
(If the bride's mother has remarried, she would use her new husband's name, *Mrs Martin Yates [or Mrs Rosemary Yates] requests the pleasure…*)

When the bride's father is host:
Mr Thomas James requests the pleasure of your company at the marriage of his daughter...

When the bride's parents are divorced and neither has remarried:
Mr Thomas James and Mrs Rosemary James request the pleasure of your company at the marriage of their daughter...

When the bride's parents are divorced and the mother has remarried:
Mr Thomas James and Mrs Rosemary Yates request the pleasure of your company at the marriage of their daughter...

When the bride's mother and stepfather are hosts:
Mr and Mrs Matthew Yates request the pleasure of your company at the marriage of her daughter...

When the bride's father and stepmother are hosts:
Mr and Mrs Thomas James request the pleasure of your company at the marriage of his daughter...

When the bride and groom are hosts themselves:
Miss Charlotte James and Mr Robert Greene request the pleasure of your company at their marriage at...

When the hosts are unrelated to the bride:
Mr and Mrs Michael Williams request the pleasure of your company at the marriage of Fiona, daughter of the late Mr and Mrs Stephen Rees...

4 Invitation to a Service of Blessing

When a marriage takes place in a civil ceremony at a register office, it can be followed by a Service of Blessing.

An invitation to a Service of Blessing can read as follows:

Mr and Mrs Daniel Reed
request the pleasure of your company
at a Service of Blessing
following the marriage
of their daughter,
Laura
to
Mr Nicholas Grey

at _____

on _____

at _____

and afterwards at _____

RSVP
[address]

5 Invitation to an Evening Reception

If additional friends are invited to the ceremony and then to an evening reception, the wording of the usual wedding invitation can be as follows, but make clear that the invitation is for the evening party only. It can be helpful to have this invitation different in size from the main invitation so it can be easily distinguished.

> Mr and Mrs James Brown
> request the pleasure of your company
> at the marriage of their daughter
> Rachel
> to
> Mr Steven Williams
> at Christ Church, Compton
> on Saturday 27 April at 2.30 p.m.
> followed by an evening reception and barn dance
> from 6.00 p.m. at Leighton Hall
>
> RSVP
> [address]

If the invitation is for the evening reception alone, it can take the form of an ordinary party invitation. Alternatively, the invitation can read:

> Mr and Mrs James Brown
> request the pleasure of your company
> at a reception
> following the marriage of their daughter
> Rachel
> to
> Mr Steven Williams
>
> at ....
> on..
> at ....
> RSVP
> [address]

6 Order of Service

The forenames or initials of the bride and groom, the name of the church and the date of the wedding may all be printed on the front of the service sheet.

Printed on the inside will be the order of service and the words of hymns, readings and prayers or other appropriate information.

ORDER OF SERVICE

At the entrance of the bride
Trumpet Voluntary   J. Clarke

HYMN
[words in full]

THE MARRIAGE

READING
1 Corinthians 13

ADDRESS
Revd Martin Stilwell

PRAYERS

HYMN
[words in full]

THE SIGNING OF THE REGISTER
During the signing of the Register
Solo

C.M. Widor: Toccata in F

7 Seasonal Guide to Flowers

All Seasons
Daisy, Freesia, Gerbera, Iris, Lily, Rose

Spring
Arum lily, Auricula, Bluebell, Foxglove, Freesia, Gardenia, Hyacinth, Lilac, Pansy, Primrose, Tulip

Summer
Delphinium, Eucryphia, Fuchsia, Gardenia, Geranium, Honeysuckle, Hydrangea, Larkspur, Lavender, Lily, Lisianthus, Marigold, Sunflower, Sweetpea

Autumn
Alstroemeria, Amaryllis, Chrysanthemum, Euphorbia, Heather, Hydrangea, Hypericum berry, Gerbera, Ivy, Orchid, Snowberry

Winter
Amaryllis, Anemone, Christmas rose, Dark red rose, Dendrobium, Eucalyptus, Fir, Holly, Hyacinth, Ivy, Jasmine, Lily, Orchid

8 Suggested Readings for a Church Wedding

Genesis 2:15–24

Psalms: 19, 34, 84, 85, 91, 121, 139:1–18

Ecclesiastes 4:9–12

Song of Solomon 8:6–7

Isaiah 40:25–31

Matthew 5:1–10

John 2:1–11

John 15:1–4, 9–17

1 Corinthians 13:1–8a

Ephesians 3:14–21

Ephesians 5:21–33

Philippians 2:1–11

Colossians 3:12–17

1 John 4:7–12, 21

9 Suggested Readings and Poems for a Civil Wedding

Poems, readings and music for civil ceremonies must not have any religious content.

Full details of poems, readings and music can be found in *Collection of Verse and Music for your Civil Marriage* published 2002 by Civil Ceremonies Limited. A few suggestions (first line only) are listed below:

A marriage… made of two fractional lives
MARK TWAIN

A walled garden Your marriage should have within it
ANON

If thou must love me, let it be for nought
ELIZABETH BARRETT BROWNING

It is not enough to love passionately
ANATOLE FRANCE

Let me not to the Marriage of true minds
WILLIAM SHAKESPEARE

Love is not breathlessness
LOUIS DE BERNIÈRES (from *Captain Corelli's Mandolin*, see page 102)

Love takes time. It needs a history of giving and receiving
BARB UPHAM

The key to love is understanding
ANON

10 Suggested Music

Suggested Hymns for Church Weddings
[first line only]

And can it be that I should gain

And did those feet in ancient time (*Jerusalem*)

Be Thou my vision, O Lord of my heart

Come down, O Love divine

Dear Lord and father of mankind

Glorious things of thee are spoken

Guide me, O thou great redeemer

I cannot tell why He whom angels worship (tune of *Londonderry Air*)

Immortal, invisible, God only wise

I vow to you my saviour/I vow to thee my country

I will sing the wondrous story

O Lord my God, when I in awesome wonder

O praise ye the Lord!

Lead us, heavenly Father, lead us

Lord for the years, your love has kept and guided

Lord of all hopefulness, Lord of all joy (same tune as 'Be Thou my vision')

Love divine, all loves excelling

Morning has broken

O strength and stay upholding all creation

Praise, my soul, the King of heaven

Praise the Lord! ye heavens adore Him

Praise to the Lord, the Almighty, the King of creation

The king of love my shepherd is

The Lord's my shepherd

Suggested Classical Music for Weddings

* = probably not allowed at a civil ceremony
R = suitable during signing of the register
IN = suitable for the entrance of the bride

The following pieces are suitable for both church and civil weddings, unless otherwise indicated:

T. Albinoni: Adagio in G Minor*   R or IN

J.S. Bach: Air on a 'G' String   IN
Jesu, Joy of Man's Desiring*   IN

L. van Beethoven: Moonlight Sonata   R or IN
Symphony No. 9 ('*Choral*', last movement)

J. Charpentier: Prelude (from *Te Deum*) (the Eurovision Song Contest theme tune!)

J. Clarke: Trumpet Voluntary (*The Prince of Denmark's March*)

E. Elgar: Organ Sonata in G*
Imperial March (first movement)
Marches 1 & 4 (from *Pomp & Circumstance*)
Nimrod (from *Enigma Variations*)   R or IN

G.F. Handel: Air & Hornpipe (from *Water Music*)
Overture, La Réjouissance and Minuet Finale (from *Music for the Royal Fireworks*)
Arrival of the Queen of Sheba (from *Solomon*)   IN
Marches (from *The Occasional Oratorio* and *Scipio*)

F. Mendelssohn: Wedding March (from *A Midsummer Night's Dream*)*   IN

E. Morricone: Gabriel's Oboe (from *The Mission*)   IN

W.A. Mozart: Wedding March (from *The Marriage of Figaro*)

J. Pachelbel: Canon in D   IN

H. Purcell: Rondeau (from *Abdelazzar*)
Trumpet Tune in D
Trumpet Tune in C (from *King Arthur*)

J. Stanley: Trumpet Voluntary in D

L. Vierne: Finale (from *Symphony I in D minor*)*

A. Vivaldi: Allegro [Spring] (from *The Four Seasons*)

R. Wagner: Bridal Chorus (from *Lohengrin*)*
Overture (from *The Mastersingers*) **IN**

W. Walton: Crown Imperial (Coronation March)
Orb and Sceptre (Coronation March)
Incidental Music (from *Richard III*)

C.M. Widor: Toccata in F (from *Symphony V for Organ*)*
Finale (from *Symphony VI for Organ*)*

Popular Music

Any popular music can also be used to personalize your civil marriage ceremony. There is a huge range of modern love songs to choose from which include:

Diana Ross: Ain't No Mountain High Enough

The Beatles: All You Need Is Love

Willie Nelson: Always on My Mind

Simon and Garfunkel: Bridge Over Troubled Water

Elton John: Can You Feel the Love Tonight?

Rod Stewart/Van Morrison: Have I Told You Lately

Olivia Newton John: Hopelessly Devoted to You

Art Garfunkel: I Only Have Eyes for You

Bill Withers: Lovely Day

The Beatles: Love Me Do

Elvis Presley: Love Me Tender

Celine Dion: My Heart Will Go On (love theme from *Titanic*)

Ben E. King: Stand By Me

Bing Crosby and Grace Kelly: True Love

Leo Sayer: When I Need You

Care for the Family

Care for the Family is a national charity committed to strengthening family life and helping those who are hurting because of family breakdown.

Since it was founded in 1988, over two hundred and fifty thousand people have attended seminars on marriage, parenting and other family issues.

International speaker, Rob Parsons is the organisation's Executive Director and is also the best-selling author of 'The Sixty Minute Father' and 'The Heart of Success'.

If you would like to hear more about our national family life events, encouragement for your family and receive help to make a difference in your community, please write to us today.

Care for the Family, PO Box 488,
Cardiff CF15 7YY, telephone (029) 2081 0800
or visit us online at www.careforthefamily.org.uk

Now you can help couples in the early years of their marriage

When the reality of married life fails to live up to their expectations, many couples are left questioning the commitment they have made.

Connect2 has been designed to help support and encourage those couples in the early years of their life together.

This unique five-session course can be run in your community and addresses issues that all newly-weds face:

1 Love for a lifetime

2 Communication and differences

3 Resolving conflict

4 Great expectations

5 Intimacy, romance and sex

Connect2 is easy-to-use, practical, fun and simple - and costs just £29.99 (plus p+p)

Order your copy by calling **(029) 2081 0800** or online at **www.careforthefamily.org.uk**

Do you want to get your marriage off to a great start?

Many engaged couples have unrealistic expectations of marriage. By spending time with a support couple you can give your marriage the best possible start.

the national
couple
support network

Helping couples to build healthy marriages

For further details contact **The National Couple Support Network** on **(029) 2081 0800** or email **ncsn@cff.org.uk**

THE MARRIAGE PREPARATION COURSE

The Marriage Preparation Course is a series of five sessions designed to help any couple develop strong foundations for a lasting marriage covering:

- Expressing feelings and learning to listen
- The importance of commitment
- Resolving conflict
- Keeping love alive and developing a fulfilling sexual relationship
- Talking about goals and values

The course has just been produced on video. Presented by Nicky and Sila Lee the programmes include interviews with married couples, animated graphics, topical reports, bible readings for weddings and street interviews. The videos allow for breaks when the couples on the course are given time to discuss various subjects on their own.

Nicky & Sila Lee have been married for over 25 years and have four children. They are on the staff of Holy Trinity Brompton.